Themself

My Experience as an Open University Creative Writing Student

JAMES KEMP

GW00776544

Other Work by James Kemp

Crisis Point (science fiction)

Copyright © 2016 James Kemp

All rights reserved.

ISBN-13: 978-1-909951-16-7

3 5 7 9 10 8 6 4 2

Castlegreen Publishing
http://www.castlegreen.org.uk/
Merstham, Surrey

DEDICATION

With thanks to my tutor and the other students on
A215 Creative Writing in 2013

CONTENTS

Table of Contents

INTRODUCTION

This is part inspirational life writing about how I learnt to write and apply some craft to my stories, and part vehicle for my writing. Mainly though I hope that you will see how I have crafted stories and poems from the examples that I have given.

Much of this book is taken from my blog, but I've presented it in a way that makes it much easier to read the interesting bits. That's from the perspective of someone who is considering studying creative writing, whether informally or at a university or college. I completed an Open University creative writing course while working full time and being a parent. It's hard work, and challenging to find time to get it done. However I enjoyed it immensely.

That course isn't the only one I've done, I'm most of the way through my second undergraduate degree, and I should finish in May 2017. After that I intend to publish my first novel, Perfects (which is at second draft stage). I've also been commissioned to write a military history of the campaigns in the three kingdoms following the Glorious Revolution.

Currently, http://www.themself.org/ has almost 500 blog posts on it spanning a 21 year time frame, one of the most popular posts is from 1995. There's a lot of words there, and only a small set of them are here too. I realise that this won't be selling my book to you. There's a lot of extra stuff in here too that I've not published anywhere else. I've also taken out a lot of ephemeral stuff and opinions on things not related to either writing or studying with the open university.

I've gone through the notes and exercises I did as part of the creative writing course and added them in at the appropriate points. I've also included some of the unpublished stories I wrote, notably my end of module assessment *Hunting Nazis*. That's a sort of X-Files meets the SOE with some unfinished business in Berlin in the early 1950s.

Part 1: Beginnings

1 - Learning about creativity

NaNoWriMo – the end
1 December 2012

So November is finished, although my draft novel isn't. I managed to write 44,463 words during November, which isn't quite the magic 50k needed to claim a win. Details of my writing progress are available from http://www.nanowrimo.org/en/participants/jmkemp/novels/exodus-331001/stats

I really enjoyed the process and it wasn't as difficult as it first appeared. Some of it is helped by the regular pep talk broadcast mails, and the stats counter tells you how many words you need to average every day that you have left to hit the magic 50k. However the pep talk mails give you a more human view of it, and I found them to be good encouragement to keep going.

So why, with all that encouragement and signposting, did I not manage to hit fifty thousand words? Well I nearly did, and this was despite starting five days late (I first wrote anything on 6th November) and only deciding on a whim to what I was going to write about. I approached this in a very literal way, I only found out what NaNoWriMo was on the evening of the 5th November, and I then dived straight in.

What lessons did I learn from this?

- writing every day isn't hard, it just needs perseverance, I ended up using my train journeys to and from work;
- I can compose, and type, text at about 30 words per minute (varied from 20-42);
- Some more planning and plotting before the start would get it moving faster;
- Starting to write on 1 November makes 50k easier to achieve (I averaged about 2k words a day, so that extra five days would have brought me in over the 50k);
- ignore the inner editor, write the story in one pass, and then go back through it to improve and re-write the bits you aren't happy with (which is what I intended to do during December and January once I've written the conclusion);
- My story won't be finished in 50k words, so I'll need to write some more;
- Writing stories down is fun, and it takes your mind off other stuff, like work;

So there you have it, I've got a 44k story that I need to go finish. When it's done I'll need to edit it a bit and then I'll make it available for other people to read. The story itself is a collective narrative, so once I've written the bits to the extent that I'm happy with them I need to chop them up and stitch them together as a single narrative that makes sense, so don't expect to see it that soon!

Have fun, and seriously, try it yourself next year. I'm setting my calendar for mid-October to come up with some ideas and pre-plan my next novel...

Creative Writing Starts Soon

23 September 2013

The next course on my Open University degree is a departure from the Business Studies focus, I'll be studying Creative Writing (course code A215). I got the course materials the other day, a big red book (affectionately known to the students of A215 as BRB); some CDs with author interviews and a study guide.

Controversially, amongst those on the forum, there is no list of TMA questions (all the usual guidance etc is there, but the core questions that tell you what is required are missing). Theories abound on whether this is to get us to engage first, or whether they are just still re-writing the TMA questions. I guess we'll find out soon enough. The course website and tutor group forums are due to open on Wednesday.

I'm looking forward to this course, for what I hope are obvious reasons if you've read the blog before. However I haven't really got down to reading the BRB because I've been using my time to try and finish off the Exodus Series so that I can focus on the course.

The other thing I want to do is collect up a list of the other students on my course with blogs and published material to make a new blog-roll for that, so that even when I cannot personally keep you entertained you might get something from others. One of the things I have noticed is that we cannot publish material that we want to use in an assignment until after that assignment has been marked, so there may well be chunks of things appearing shortly after assignments have been sent back to us!

Here are the A215 student blogs I've found so far:

- http://www.connbardi.com/ Conn Bardi
- http://readingwritingeverything-heather.blogspot.co.uk/
- http://hjmusk.wordpress.com/
- http://bexmills.wix.com/boogies-banter
- http://www.emmylva.blogspot.com/
- http://dragonmusing.wordpress.com/
- http://isabelj327.blogspot.co.uk/ Isabel Johnstone
- http://www.arriettysfootprints.wordpress.com
- http://yappinandyarnin.blogspot.co.uk Janet Daly
- http://randomwordiness.wordpress.com

2 - Exercises

Writing Routines
26 September 2013

This is inspired as a short piece from a question on the A215 (Creative writing) student forum about what discipline people apply to their writing.

I write as part of my work, although mostly not for publication these days (I've had posts in the past where some of my output was made public). The last public work I did was a guest blog entry for the Government Digital Service on Learning from Service Assessments (http://digital.cabinetoffice.gov.uk/2013/08/08/learning-from-assessments/).

On the other hand I also write for my own enjoyment, and lots of that is made public, mainly blog entries here, although I also write fiction and have published some of the Exodus Series recently. Last year I joined in National Novel Writing Month (see http://www.nanowrimo.org/) (it runs every November – affectionately known as NaNoWriMo to its participants). That challenge of writing 50k words in a month got me into the habit of writing most days.

My writing time is the commute to and from work. That isn't my ideal time to do writing, but it is the only time I can't do anything else with. At home I try and spend time with my family, which includes time as a school governor and a section assistant for my son's beaver colony. At work things are full on, I have multiple projects to manage and lots of meetings to attend, lunch isn't usually a break.

The commute involves a 15 minute walk from my house to the train station. I use that time to think through the plot points and the scene that I want to write next. Sometimes I rehearse the dialogue in my head, replaying the conversations until either I get to the station, or I'm completely happy with it.

I live just outside the M25, and most days I manage to get a seat on the train with a table. On those days I then spend the 35 minutes or so typing furiously (using Scrivener produced by Literature & Latte https://www.literatureandlatte.com/scrivener.php) to get the story out of my head and into the computer. Mostly I manage about 7-800 words on the way into work. If there are delays then there can be more than that. On Tuesday I wrote 2,200 words on the two way journey.

I also have a 10-15 minute walk between the station and my office, so there is thinking time possible there. The process is repeated on the way home.

Editing is also done on the train to and from work, and in the gaps from other travel. On occasion I travel for work and if so I spend the evenings afterwards either editing or writing if I stay anywhere overnight. That's pretty rare though, as I prefer to go home if it is possible.

Some Writing Exercises

Think of a specific place you love, a physical location such as a particular city, landscape, house, garden. For your chosen place, record the sounds, textures, odours, flavours and objects you would find there. Use imagination or memory when writing your descriptions. Keep the list specific and as concrete as possible. Also keep descriptions imaginative and interesting--for example--instead of: I hear a bird calling, you might write, I hear a young starling shuffling in its nest. Keep your writing to about 200 words.

Write down three things for each of the following:

- sounds that you can hear;
- textures that you can feel;
- odours that you can smell;
- flavours that you can taste;
- objects that you can see.

My answers

Write down three things for each of the following:

- sounds that you can hear;
  1. up above the traffic helicopter keeps an eye on the ebb and flow of the motorway
  2. the great tits sing in the bushes to warn each other of the predatory magpies keeping watch for their next meal
  3. the gentle susurration of the motorway traffic blows in the wind as the cars pass between Gatwick and the M25
- textures that you can feel;
  1. underfoot the clay soil clings to shoes, and I slide away where it is wet.
  2. Long grass brushes ankles and shins and washes them with morning dew
  3. the hard rough edge of the concrete path tickles bare feet, and warms them in the summer sun

- odours that you can smell;
  1. After it rains there is a verdant edge to the cleaned air tinged with damp leaf mould
  2. In summer, the tang of woodsmoke tickles the back of the nose
  3. from the kitchen there comes the fragrance of cake baking in the oven, and promising a tasty afternoon tea when the gardening is done.
- flavours that you can taste;
  1. barbecued lamb spits and sizzles on the grill, and then its juices flow in the mouth
  2. fresh strawberries picked from the plant give a sharp, acid edge to their red sweetness
  3. Coffee, black as tar but only mildly bitter at the edges despite its potency because it has been cold brewed
- objects that you can see.
  1. A wooden fence hides the farmyard, although the corrugated steel barn towers above it
  2. Down the sides of the garden there are many trees, oak, fir, sycamore, beech, cherry, ash, apple, plum, rose and some decorative ones I do not yet know the names of.
  3. Taking up much of the green centre is a large 14 foot trampoline, with a plastic slide as its entry and exit. It shares the grassy area with a play house, two swings, a sandpit, water table, tunnel and assorted balls and plastic furniture.

Commentary

At first this seems a bit of a strange exercise. It is relatively straightforward describing what you can see and hear, but smells and tastes are much harder to describe with words.

When I think about conversation about things, usually we explain those with reference to other smells, rather than trying to break them down with adjectives. Even where that is common (for example with wines) we see that as being rather too creative and poncy.

The other thing that seemed a bit odd was coming up with exactly three things. For most of the categories one or two were really easy, but the second or third item was difficult, especially when it was smells and tastes.

I chose my garden, it has a couple of smells, although my sense of smell is usually impaired because I have asthma and often my nose is blocked (when it isn't I have a very acute sense of smell, and can often pick out things others cannot).

Tastes for the garden were much more difficult, because I don't usually eat there, although I do often take my coffee there when I'm doing gardening.

Picking a Memory

When you have completed the list of sensory perceptions, write specifically about a personal memory you have associated with the place that you chose for the first exercise. Focus just on one moment and root it in the specific place by using your list of senses. Keep it relatively short.

Using the present tense write about a personal memory of either a place or a character in your notebook. Make it brief, 200ish words, but try to get as many sensory perceptions as possible going, and try to fix the memory in time, so that it is a single moment. Include details and don't be afraid of uncertainties.

My Answer

It is Sunday afternoon and I am in my back garden with my wife and two children. The younger is 17 months old and she is exploring the corners of the garden, babbling and shouting with the sheer excitement of being outside on a fine autumn day. The elder, a boy of almost eight, is busying himself collecting sticks, because we are building a den together. He has decided that he wants a survival shelter at the bottom of the garden.

Together we patrol the garden looking for long poles of Ash in the hedgerows and the margins. Each time we find one the hand saw comes out and he enthusiastically saws at the bottom the selected branch while I hold it steady. When his arms tire, or his enthusiasm wanes, I take over and rapidly remove the branch. Together we drag the foliage to the back of the garden where we strip the longer thicker poles of leaves and side shoots. He very carefully uses the sharp knife bought for whittling pieces of wood.

Although he has had practice with this for almost a year, the rules are very clear, he can only use a sharp tool when directly under adult supervision. Patiently he trims the leaves all the way along the longer pole. We divide up cutting off the side branches according to their size. I take the larger ones with an orange pair of long handled loppers, he uses the same tool on the smaller ones where his size and strength allow him to do so safely.

Once we've got half a dozen like that we lash them together with garden string. He cuts the pieces of string with the knife and then directs me where to tie the poles together. To an outsider it would look like he has done this before, but the reality is that I'm the one that has.

Commentary

Once you start going with the memory it is hard to keep the word count down. Partly this is because I did it immediately on the back of the first exercise. Having spent some time thinking about my garden and listing three things for each of the main categories, and in particular using the sort of language that was suggested, it made it much easier to bring a vivid memory into mind.

Having a richer level of detail in my mind meant that it was relatively easy to write a descriptive present tense passage in a few minutes.

This step (above) is a good exercise in blurring the edges between fiction and reality. By focusing on one place and having already noted down the details of this place and a memory associated with it, this step allows you to fictionalise the place in a way that shifts the narrative into a new frame, that of a story.

Five Facts

Taking the same place that you have used for the first two exercises, write down five facts about it. These can be used to help you turn the sense and the memory into a piece of fiction.

My Answers

1.   70 years ago my garden was a farmer's field (the barn is still on the other side of the fence)

2.   As far as I know we are the second family to live in the house

3.   The previous family moved into the house in 1957 and had one son, the mother was a tax inspector, we don't know what the father did and the son now lives in Birmingham. They weren't originally from the London area, but came here for work. The mother was in her late 80s when she died in 2004, so she would have been born before 1920, making her an adult during the war.

4.   During the war an American Bomber crashed into the side of Reigate Hill. The first person on the scene was someone with the same name as the woman that lived in our house (and the same age, too much to be a coincidence). She found one of the crew still alive, but dying, and stayed with him to comfort him.

5.   The house was built in 1957 by the County of London Authority as part of the rehousing of people bombed out. There is a butler's sink buried in the garden with just the rim showing above the soil level. Sometimes we find bricks buried in the garden away from the house when we are planting things.

What if?

Thinking about the five facts above, give them a twist. What if you have mis-understood, or not quite been given the full facts?

My answer

What if Mrs Edwards wasn't a tax inspector, but instead her war work was in intelligence. Perhaps her husband also did that line of work. He could have been serving overseas while she was in the HQ in the Greater London area, Reigate is only a short train ride from central London (it is why we chose to live there).

What if it the field that became my back garden was the closest to the farmhouse, and was used for stashing valuables in the event of invasion. There were lots of defences built in summer 1940. The farmer might have been in the Home Guard and had a secret cache built where our garden now is.

One of our elderly neighbours commented that there was a special tree in our garden, but didn't say which one. Maybe it was planted to mark the cover of a secret cache? It might have valuables in it, or weapons, or perhaps explosives that have become unstable

Turning it into a story

Use all of the answers above to write a very short story, dont worry overly about the word count, or even around crafting the words. Just write a little piece of fiction, a single scene that has something happen in it. Draw on your answers for the four exercises.

Short Fiction – Planting the Past
12 October 2013

This is a piece of short fiction written for the first online tutorial of A215 Creative Writing. It followed three exercises intended to spur creativity (see above). The exercises centred around thinking of a place that you love being and then asked questions about that place.

The first was some descriptive writing about the place, things you could see, smell, hear etc.

The second was to write about a flash memory in the present tense and the last was to list some facts about the place and then spin off some 'what if...' questions related to those facts.

This last one was what really got my 400 word piece of fiction going. So here it is, all 400 words of it.

Planting the Past
Hands resting on her heavily pregnant belly, Dot could feel her baby kicking. Her husband leant on a spade, sweat glistening on his brow and mud clay sticking to the soles and sides of his old army boots. Boots that he now only wore for gardening.

They were home for good now, in their own house, with their own garden. She had enjoyed the travel, and the adventure of it all, even the fear and danger. Even though she'd looked death square in the face more than once, and been close enough to feel the last breath of more than one unfortunate person, she'd tell you that she'd had a good war.

Today was a funeral for that past, which would be mourned by them both. The box lay on the grass, two feet long and ten inches on the shorter sides. It was still the same dull green, with stencil letters, as when she'd first seen it at the aerodrome. For years it lived in Reggie's car, ready just in case. Even with rationing they'd always had petrol. Her job needed her to drive, and Reggie's record counted for quite a bit too.

Now that was all over, it was over ten years since the war, although they'd been needed more than ever since it finished. In the bushes the great tits sang their courtship songs and overhead a magpie soared looking for prey. Other than that the only other sound was the metal spade scraping against the clay soil as Reggie squared off the hole. It was way too big for the tree that stood potless waiting to be planted.

'That'll do, I reckon' said Reggie, planting his spade into the spoil heap next to the hole.

'It should.' said Dot.

Reggie unfolded some oiled cloth and laid it out on the ground. He placed the box diagonally on the centre of it before wrapping it in the cloth. His large fingers covered in reddish-brown clay confidently tied knots in the garden twine.Stepping closer Dot watched as he lay the neat parcel gently into the hole.

'What if we need to dig it up later?' Dot asked.

'Don't worry, I'm going to plant the tree to the side of it.' Reggie said, indicating a shallower part of the hole.

'I'm going inside to sit down.' said Dot.

~

'Is it done?' Dot asked.

'Yes, the cherry tree is planted.'

Commentary

It was relatively easy to write the short piece of fiction having done the exercises, but without those exercises it is unlikely I would have had the creative spark that produced that particular story. It was a very good illustration, through doing, of how one can 'force' creativity through recall of the familiar.

The first exercise in descriptive writing helped sharpen the pencil to allow it to draw more interesting pictures than it might have without the exercise, and it also gave some particular descriptions that were dropped into the fiction fragment.

The second exercise showed how you can take a specific memory and use it to create a well described passage that recounts a single moment. That in turn shows how you can draw things from memory and put them into words.

Combined with the descriptive turn from the first exercise makes for a vivid picture of the scene.

The last exercise was the one that struck the spark that lit the fire. Listing known knowns and then extrapolating from them into plausible speculation gave me a leap into the characters and the scene that I then wrote.

3 - First Assignment

A215 TMA01 – Night Patrol
13 November 2013

Here is the text I submitted for the Creative Writing assignment. The first part is unaltered. I have lightly edited Part 2 based on the feedback received (in net terms I added five words). Part 1 is a freewrite, intended to spark ideas based on a prompt. Part 2 is, in my case, a piece of autobiographical writing (my apologies if anyone recognises the events in question).

Part 1: Freewrite on prompt 'Walking at Night'
Some of the most fun I ever had was wandering about in the dark. As a teenager I used to play outside at night, walking through the streetlights, with others playing hide and seek in the dark corners. It taught me to move silently and to use shadows to sneak back to the lamp-post we used as the home base.

Later I put those skills to a different use wandering British Army training areas armed to the teeth and looking for trouble. Everything was secured so that it wouldn't rattle, money was left behind, loose bits of equipment tied or taped down using dark green paracord, black electrician's tape or black gaffer tape depending on what it was. When I was done I would jump up and down and shake my body like there was a disco thumping, all the while listening for rattles, squeaks and rustles.

Preparations complete I would go with the rest of the patrol into the dark. The landscape always looks different at night, especially without lights. Crossing a wide open field is very hard, landmarks can usually only be made out a few yards ahead, even in bright moonlight the horizons are a lot closer than in daylight.

Part 2: Autobiographical writing 'Night Patrol'

I'm on point for the patrol. The countryside renders in dark blue and grey, lit by stars and a sliver of moon. The horizon is close, sky and grass blend together less than 100 metres away. Trees stand darkly, visible further out. We move in foot long grass parallel to a track, avoiding waist high patches of thick, jagged gorse.

Each step is slow and deliberate. My left foot moves forwards. Toes gently touch the ground before I place the rest of my foot down. I slowly pass my weight from right leg to left as I scan the vague horizon. I listen carefully. My full attention is to the front, others behind me are watching to the left, right and rear.

We move silently and without lights. It's November, we're just outside Inverness and the air smells icily fresh. The breeze cools my face. Moving makes me overheat because of the weight I carry, 30 pounds of food, water and ammunition round my waist, my combat jacket laden with chocolate, notebook, torch, knife, whistle and more ammo. I'm wearing multiple layers, t-shirt, shirt, jersey, combat jacket, scarf, woollen hat, helmet and two pairs of gloves. These are unavoidable, we may lie in ambush for hours.

Ahead the ground undulates, which means we're close to the trenches. The spoil is camouflaged with turf, but it stands proud of the surroundings. A barbed wire entanglement resolves itself ten metres in front, the wire only apparent when I can touch it.

The patrol commander produces white mine tape from his jacket. He ties some to the barbed wire as we skirt around it. In the gap, I spot a hair thin trip-wire stretching blackly across my path. One end is on the stake holding a corner of the entanglement, the other lost in the dark.

I wave the patrol into cover before carefully placing more white tape over the trip-wire. I follow it and find a flare on a post. I want to deactivate the flare, but the patrol commander shakes his head. We mark the trip-wire and pass the patrol over it.

A few metres further on I see sandbags atop the nearest hillock. Another silent hand signal and we form a line. Moments later a soldier is highlighted on our skyline. Looking around I observe three other trenches.

I hold a thunderflash prominently for the patrol to see. The commander next to me does the same, and together we pull the strikers. It sounds like a giant match being struck, but doesn't seem to attract any reaction. I throw mine in a great arc to land near the closest trench.

As it leaves my hand I count in my head. I re-take control of my rifle. I get to four. Lightning flashes accompanied by a tremendous bang. The patrol starts shooting. The night air now smells of burnt carbon and fireworks.

There are shouts of "Stand To!". We've taken them by surprise. Return fire pops and crackles all across the position, not just the trenches closest to us. Most don't appear to know where we are. I can see muzzle flashes of the closer firers.

Each shot is accompanied by a blue flash, and I can tell that they aren't pointed at me. I hear several flares hiss up and burst with a soft pop. A series of short-lived, cold suns brighten the neighbourhood. Sharp, moving shadows subside as they drift downwards on a parachute. Clear fire orders can be heard and the shooting slows slightly.

Surprise over, we leave in reverse order. While I provide covering fire, a comrade runs into the tripwire we marked and gets tangled. Three others bunch round to help. I hear inventive swearing and the flare fizzing. I close one eye to preserve my night vision, they are clearly silhouetted. Before following I find a smoke grenade and pull the pin. I check the breeze, release the lever and lob it to obscure my departure.

Speed is now more important than stealth. I charge past my friends, beyond the flare light, throwing myself onto the ground. I fire a few times until they thunder past me. The commander shouts to regroup at the lone tree. I sprint after them. When I get to the tree there is a feeling of exhilaration. Clouds of steam show how much exercise we've done. Behind us there is still shooting. I pull a water bottle from my belt, it is chilled as though from the fridge and it tastes sweet.

Reflective commentary

Free writing is new to me, I hadn't previously written from a prompt. Usually I have an idea for a story, I think about it and then type. The free write shown here is a straight first draft, and I stopped when I got to the requisite word count. It triggered memories of 25+ years ago when I regularly walked in the dark.

I originally tried to write some fiction based on the freewrite. I took a piece that I had written for the online tutorial and tried to see how I could use the techniques learnt in the tutorial.

I wrote about 400 words but decided that the link to the freewrite was tenuous. So I decided to try writing what I knew, and wrote an autobiographical piece that directly flowed from the freewrite.

While writing it I consciously tried to describe the scene in terms of sight, sound, smell and hearing as per exercise 3.3 in the coursebook. The first draft came out at almost double the required word count, however reading it back I felt that I could edit it to fit.

I posted the first draft of Part 1 & Part 2 on the Forum in the hope of getting some feedback. There was one response, which made some suggestions which I directly incorporated into a second draft.

As well as those suggestions I re-ordered some paragraphs to make the narrative flow better, re-wrote it into present tense and removed repetition and superfluous words as per the feedback from the online tutorial. This brought the draft down to just over 800 words, which although on the high end was within the tolerance allowed.

I then posted this revised draft on the forum in case there was any further feedback. A few days later I then re-edited to make it shorter still, testing each word for necessity.

Creative Writing First Assignment Marked
12 November 2013

Today I got my marks for my first assignment on A215 Creative Writing. I'm not allowed to post the question nor the feedback. However unusually this course has an exemption from publishing my own work. Presumably because it is unlikely to help anyone else with the assignment in the future.

Creative Writing is quite different from the other academic courses that I have completed. For a start there is a limit to what you can get externally to answer the question. When I did strategy I was able to go and read loads of papers and books on the topic in addition to the course materials. For A215 the support of other people seems to take that place, along with copious redrafting. I went through more versions of this than I did with most of my academic essay writing. Also I really had no idea how good or bad it was, where I always knew for the academic essays.

The result was a good one, comfortably in the second highest band. The tutor feedback was helpful.

Part 2 – Fiction

4 - Learning about fiction

A215 Short Fiction: A Creation Myth
15 November 2013

I need to write a short story for my next assignment. Rather than racking my brains, I've been going back over stuff I'd written, but not finished, for inspiration. I'll do the exercises to see what sparks too.

I looked through my role-playing archives and found a fantasy game I ran where I'd created the setting myself rather than using a published one. There are about 17k words on this, and on top of that a stack of index cards. I was rather taken by the creation myth I wrote for the primary god in a theocracy.

Daprav
It is important to distinguish between Daprav Himself and the Church, which forms the bulk of his worshippers. Daprav is an active paternalistic God by inclination. He favours wandering amongst his people in disguise, perhaps to keep an eye on them. He is also known for speaking to His prophets in the heart of their soul, although He is not above manifesting should those prophets need a major miracle performing.

The worshippers of Daprav don't have faith, they have knowledge. The evidence of His existence is a daily phenomenon. His priests work many miracles and are enjoined to look after the flock, tending the ill and feeding the hungry. This is tempered with an injunction on the people to obey the word of Daprav, and by extension of the priesthood.

In the beginning...
Daprav is the creator of the world and all the things in it. He did this a very long time ago and spent many millennia wandering through it revelling in the beauty of his creation. He taught the early men a great deal and established many temples, each bearing slight differences according to the aspects he displayed to the tribe that built the temple. However all men were one in their devotion to Daprav and he was able to ensure that there was no strife.

One day, whilst hunting with the Obor Tribe in the great fastness of the Green Forest, Daprav came across an enchanted grove. This intrigued Him as He had not enchanted the grove, nor had any of the priests empowered with His miracles. Entering the grove He called out to its enchanter. From behind a tree stepped a powerful sorcerer. Daprav commanded him to speak.

"I am known as Hapt and I was born to work magic".

Others also stepped out from behind other trees numbering thirteen in total. They also spake their names:

"Temed, the giver of gifts" a female holding a box;

"Mistear, an archer of great repute" a slim young woman knocking an arrow to her longbow;

"Miral, the killer of many" an older male with many scars on his body and a huge axe;

"Dado, an enchanter, I created this grove" a bearded man in white robes with a golden sickle;

"Fabrius, also a creator of magics" a youth short in stature and stocky with it;

"Eubulus, a singer of songs and a teller of tales" a young man in patched clothes, holding a set of pipes;

"Aulos, the healer of wounds" a woman wearing white with braided blonde hair;

"Horin, the lover of all" a full-breasted woman with red lips and a jar of wine;

"Mousai, protector of the innocent" a man clad in armour from head to foot;

"Drok, the joker" a mischievous looking youngster dressed all in red;

"Valdese, a brave and gallant warrior" tall, dark and handsome, a man to break the hearts of many a maiden, and to carry off the souls of men in battle;

"Ojibwa, a thief and a damned good one" a medium sized woman with a lithe look to her movements as she stepped out from behind the tree.

"Why have you enchanted this grove? And why are you all here?" Daprav asked.

"We want to be Gods, and you have the means to make that so." Answered Hapt who appeared to be their leader. "We are the foremost amongst our kind and desire to share your divinity. Will you give it to us?".

"No. This cannot be so. You must go from here and forever banish any thought of elevating yourselves to godhood".

"If you will not co-operate then we shall take it from you."

And with that the thirteen worked their magic as they had planned. They cast a spell on Daprav the like of such has never before or since been seen. Their careful preparations however went awry. Instead of stealing the Divinity from Daprav they instead put him into an endless slumber. They were able to visit the world as spirits and speak unto the people, but were banished as punishment for attempting to make themselves Gods.

Had Daprav not been sent into a deep sleep He would have been able to counter their dealings with the various tribes and prevent the strife that was to come to His perfect creation. Each of the thirteen brought their own gift to the world, and with it some corruption of the people. Over the years the tribes formed their own sects and religions as the memory of Daprav was corrupted and forgotten. In time all living people had forgotten of Daprav's very existence. However He continued to exist, trapped in the sacred grove.

After about two millennia the growth of the tribes had reduced the Green Forest to a fraction of its former size and brought the grove from the depths to its very edge. He appeared in a dream to His prophet Reatham who was sleeping nearby. Reatham was a hunter and Daprav placed images of plentiful game in his dreams along with clues to the location of the grove. Reatham found his way to the grove and woke Daprav.

After the long hibernation Daprav was weak and required sustenance to build His strength back. However with neither followers nor temples He could not gain strength from sacrifices. Reatham went out amongst the people and preached to them about the goodness of Daprav. However not all was well with the world. The spirits of the thirteen were still strong and afraid that an awakened Daprav would take revenge on them stirred up the people to act against Daprav's supporters.

Reatham was killed by an angry mob incited by the spirit of Miral. The mob were persuaded that Reatham was enthralled by an evil spirit that meant to destroy the livelihood of the town. It was all Daprav could do to avoid being torn apart himself. After escaping from the mob He travelled about the world gradually building up strength and itinerant followers one by one. After some time He spoke to Rontium and commanded that he feed the poor and homeless in his district and to tell them that the food came from Daprav.

Strengthened by the prayers of the faithful Daprav regained some of His powers and perform minor miracles. Many of the worshippers didn't realise that He was the deity and instead thought Him to be a priest of Daprav, so diminished was His power. One believer who saw Him truly was Anley, a lay healer. She helped and healed the sick in His name. This boosted His following still further and in time restored more of His powers.

It was about this time that the worship of Daprav became the main religion in the small town of Balham, now known as Templeton. With the growth of His following He was able to stand up to the spirits of the thirteen and make overt use of His powers to protect Balham. It was about this time that the Duke of the District was persuaded by the spirit of Miral to destroy Balham and kill all of the people living there. He gathered his forces and attacked the town.

Daprav called down a lightning bolt from the heavens and smote the Duke from his saddle. Many of the disheartened troops fled, although others switched sides and pledged their allegiance to Daprav, including Earl Shabas who vowed his life to the God to atone for his previous wrongs against the people of Daprav. Daprav heard the oath and granted him the name of Sir Waldo with His blessing and the ability to heal the wounds of others simply by laying his hands on the afflicted part. Sir Waldo went on to lead his men to glory in the wars of independence that the Church of Daprav fought with those misguided by the spirits.

Writing and Tension/Conflict

25 November 2013

I've been working my way through the Big Red Book (BRB) that supports the Open University's A215 Creative Writing course. I've just got to the Chapter on structure and it has made me think about how to get tension and conflict into my stories.

In particular I was thinking about how to write the sort of scenes that make you want to keep on reading and keep people up at night to see what happens next. I also found this writing resource post on tension vs conflict in writing.

(http://writershelpingwriters.net/2013/11/conflict-vs-tension-2/)

The thought process that these triggered reminded me of an incident from my late teens. In July 1991 I spent a couple of weeks on the Isle of Lewis with my UOTC on annual camp. One night we were sent out on an orienteering exercise in the dark. It wasn't dark for long, at that time of year there is only about three hours of darkness up there.

There was a twist to this exercise, we had to collect parts of a military radio as we visited the grid references. When we'd done that we needed to put a call out to organise our lift home. Each group had four teams, with about eight officer cadets in each section. My section, which was leaderless (or leaderful depending on your point of view) had the task of collecting the furthest away radio.

Two other sections needed to find their radio and RV in the middle somewhere. The fourth section was operating out of the camp we were staying in. The grandly titled RAF Stornoway was a collection of Nissen huts overlooking the runway at Stornoway airport. We would end up about 20km from the camp.

Being July it wasn't overly cold, and we were dropped off about 2300 for the walk. There was 100% cloud cover, and a light wind. There were only four collection points, all within a kilometre or so of the previous one.

Despite this, I carried all my usual belt kit with water bottle, brew kit, first aid kit, snacks and a waterproof. Most of the rest of the section told me I was crazy to lug all that stuff when it wasn't needed. There was about 20lbs of kit round my waist (I had dumped the bricks that kept it to the 35lbs I needed for training runs).

We set off in the evening twilight and found the first cache quite quickly. The others followed suit, it took us about an hour to collect together the radio. I was designated as the signaller because I had the most experience, and so I assembled and carried it. By this time it was thoroughly dark, and we needed to find our way to a lay-by on a road where we could call for someone to come and pick us up.

There were no landmarks visible because the cloud cover stopped the starlight from making the ground visible and the area is very rural. However we could see a lit farmhouse window in the middle distance, and we rationalised that it would be on the roadway. From there all we needed to do was follow the road to the lay-by. So off we set in a straight line to the house.

In the intervening space we crossed three wire fences and a burn. None of these were clear until we were a couple of metres or so from them, but all were visible enough when we were on top of them. When we were about half-way to the farmhouse we came across another fence, which we duly crossed.

Almost as soon as we were over it there was a second fence in front of us. We noted that the ground underfoot was packed down and covered with animal tracks. It must be a track with a fence on both sides.

We crossed the second fence. As we went to carry on there was a third fence. When we were at the third fence we were unable to see the first fence, and could very hazily make out the fourth when we crossed it. At the fourth, there was a fifth, and then a sixth.

I lost count of how many fences we crossed, but eventually we ran out of fences and then had a clear walk to the roadway. A daylight inspection showed us that we'd hit the middle of some sheep pens. Had the visibility had been better we might have seen the edges and been able to go round.

The relevance of this to writing?

Well, I think there always ought to be some new obstacle or conflict every time you resolve something, but all the while there should be the central guiding light (like the farmhouse window) that directs the characters to their long term goal.

Writing Exercise – Lovesick Witch

7 December 2013

I'm in the middle of a 10 day online tutorial for A215 Creative Writing (not continuously for ten days, thankfully, but in little bits posted to the tutor group forum over a ten day period). So the first task was to create a character randomly based on two lists, one of traits/conditions and the other of occupations. Being a gamer I rolled dice to choose my combination and got 'Lovesick Witch'. So here are the 200 words (199 actually) that I wrote to show that character (the rules being that it needed to be show in third person, rather than a descriptive tell and that we needed to avoid stereotypes).

Lovesick Witch

Her phone still had no updates. When he'd smiled at her, she felt warm inside. She'd re-read the message asking if she wanted to meet him for coffee more times than she could remember. Then she had read all of his social media profiles. It was ridiculous, she couldn't wait for him, he'd never call. No, she had to go and woo him.

The cat mewled at her as she pushed it from her lap and stood. She tucked the phone into the front pocket of her tight black levis before loping towards a bookcase with a glint in her grey eyes. Her hands went straight to an old hardback book with a faded spine at waist height. Pulling it from the shelf she flicked through the contents pages. Finding what she wanted she turned through the book, one hand held the book while the other played with a strand of blonde hair that dangled down the side of her face. A smile built across her face as she read.

'Gotcha!' she said, snapping the book closed.

In the kitchen she gathered ingredients, a small silver bowl and a couple of candles.

The phone buzzed 'Starbucks at eight?'

Writing Exercise – Bored Athlete meets Lovesick Witch
11 December 2013

The second part of the online tutorial for the creative writing course (A215 from the Open University) was to take the character that I made up in the first part (the lovesick witch) and then write a dialogue scene where she met one of the other characters.

I had a choice of two others, either of which would have made a good scene. I chose the bored athlete because one of the other students had already posted a meeting between the lovesick witch and the introvert adolescent.

The target word count was 200 and most of it needed to be dialogue, no more than a third for scene setting. I broke that last rule a bit, but think it still works. So here it is.

Bored Athlete meets Lovesick Witch
Walking home through the park, some young men racing on the track caught Willow's eye. One of them effortlessly ahead of the others. He was tall and muscled, and as he thudded down the track towards her she could see his face twisted in a delicious frown. His blue eyes were cold, but there was a glint of satisfaction there. She detested self-obsessed sporty people, but this man was different.

He bounced to a halt in front of her, he'd seen her watching him. She was wearing tight black clothing that showed off her body, about a foot shorter than him, blonde, and interesting. The others also came to a stop behind him, he could hear their exhausted panting.

'Enjoy the show?' he said. He wasn't even out of breath.

'Remarkable. You run like Bolt' she replied.

'You're a fan?'

'Not really, but you couldn't miss the Olympics. It was compelling even though I don't really like sports.'

'Me neither.'

Willow laughed, he was definitely a handsome young man, and witty with it.

'I'm Dave, by the way.' He said, holding out his hand with a smile.

'Willow.' She took it and looked him in the eye as she did so. Her perfume hit him, a spicy flower that hit some hard-wired buttons inside him. Her interest rate had just turned up to 11.

They stood silently for a moment.

Dave let go of Willow's hand.

A215 Notebook Entry – Modern Witches
5 January 2014

I wrote the notebook entry pictured below in support of the story I've written for TMA02 of the Open University A215 Creative Writing course I'm doing at the moment. While it was mostly written from memory it was evolving the role of 'cunning folk' as explained by several books on my 17th century bookshelf that I don't have time to properly reference (not least because I wrote this from memory and without re-consulting books I read some years ago for the most part).

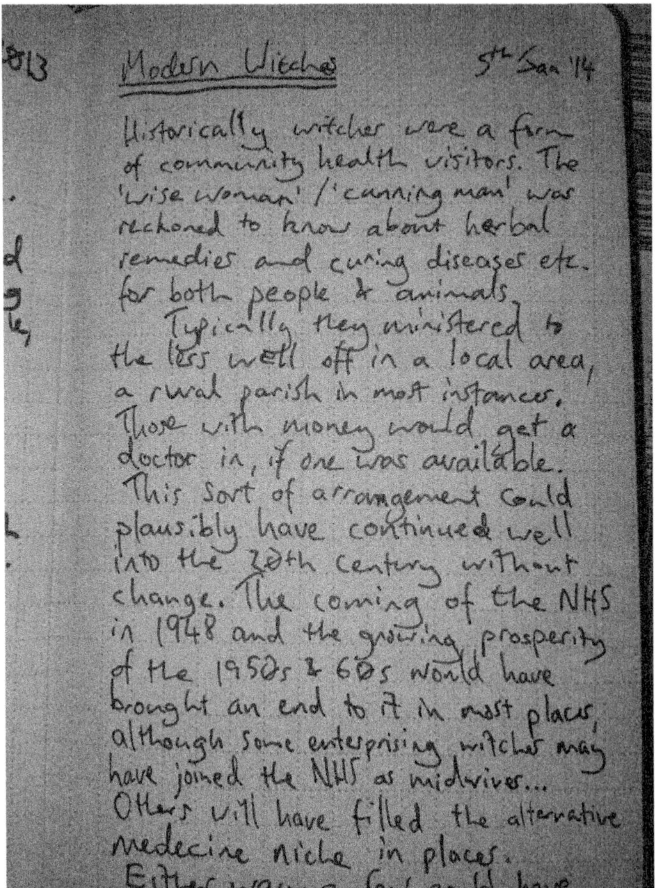

Modern Witches 5th Jan '14

Historically witches were a form of community health visitors. The 'wise woman' / 'cunning man' was reckoned to know about herbal remedies and curing diseases etc. for both people & animals.

Typically they ministered to the less well off in a local area, a rural parish in most instances. Those with money would get a doctor in, if one was available.

This sort of arrangement could plausibly have continued well into the 20th century without change. The coming of the NHS in 1948 and the growing prosperity of the 1950s & 60s would have brought an end to it in most places, although some enterprising witches may have joined the NHS as midwives... Others will have filled the alternative medicine niche in places.

Either way, a few could have

An entry from my writer's notebook on modern witches

5 - Second Assignment

A215 – TMA02 – Rounds
24 January 2014

This is the story as submitted for the second assignment on the Open University A21 Creative Writing course, before revision to improve it in line with the tutor feedback.

Rounds
Alice clipped the name badge onto her uniform before picking up her keys. First stop today was Granny Jack's house. She needed advice before visiting Fiona, her childhood friend.

Outside it was a warm, dry spring day. Daffodils bloomed and the hedge had lost its clipped rectangular shape. Alice's car was parked on the narrow roadway outside her terraced cottage. She opened the boot with her key and checked the contents of her bag before taking it out and locking up behind. She strode off along the road, swinging the bag as she went.

Granny Jack was the oldest living resident of Lower Harwood. She lived alone on the ground floor of a row of cottages. Her vegetable patch was turning green with weeds. Washing hung on the line, the grass under it unkempt.

Alice knocked and then let herself in. She walked down the short corridor, calling 'Granny, it's me, Alice!' as she went. The living room had a fire going in the grate, Alice couldn't recall visiting when there wasn't, and on each side of the fireplace was an easy chair. The far corner held the door to the kitchen, where Granny stood wearing her apron and with flour covering her hands.

'Hello dear, how are you?' asked Granny.

'I'm fine Granny, I just came round to say hello.' Said Alice.

'On your way to work I see?' Granny looked pointedly at the bag and uniform.

'Well, I was just walking by. I need to go see Fiona later on.' Alice said.

Granny raised an eyebrow. 'Your friend from school?'

'Yes, she's expecting twins, but there are complications. You know the family history don't you?'

'Do you have time for some tea?' asked Granny. 'The pot's ready'.

'I'd love some, please.'

Alice followed Granny into the kitchen, where a large teapot stood on the hob. Granny poured tea for Alice.

'Thanks, Granny. How are you?'

'I'm fine, dear' Granny said. 'Although the garden needs some looking after.'

'I noticed. Has Davie not been round recently?'

'No, dear, he doesn't want to see Rachel, not after Henry's twenty-first.'

'From what I saw then, I thought they'd got on very well'

'Oh, they did, but that was the problem.'

'How sad.'

'Don't worry, they'll see sense, but until they do I haven't got anyone to do my garden.'

Alice realised that Granny wouldn't tell her anything until Alice had arranged someone to do Granny's garden. Leaving Granny's house she thought about calling on Rachel upstairs, then remembered that Rachel would be at work. Alice closed the gate behind her and went towards the surgery. As she walked she considered who else might help. Turning the corner onto Stuart Street she saw Billy Fleming digging his garden.

'Hello, Billy, how are you?' Alice called.

'Oh, hi!' Billy replied.

'You're doing well with your garden, it looks nice.'

'Ach, it's no bad, but I fair enjoy having a go at it. Keeps me out of mischief.'

'Oh, it's better than not bad. I think you're pretty handy as a gardener.'

'Thanks, I suppose I'd better get on with it then.'

'Um, could you help my Granny out with her garden?'

'Is it no Davie that does that?'

'Not any more.'

'I'd love tae help, but I need to watch the bairn when the ex-wife's at work.'

'If I got a babysitter could you manage it?'

'Oh aye. Nae problem.'

'Thanks. I'll come back and see you later.' Alice replied, giving Billy a big smile.

The next stop was easy, her friend's sister Dianne lived across the road from the surgery. She could pop in and get Dianne to baby-sit. Alice carried on, Stuart

Street was a short link road, and she soon reached the corner to the main road where the shops were. The surgery lay on a back street just past the churchyard.

Alice stopped outside a semi-detached house surrounded by garden. The drive was empty, but the windows were open. Alice walked round to find Mrs Dowding hanging out her washing.

'Hello Alice, what brings you round?' she asked.

'Is Dianne around, someone wanted a baby-sitter?' Alice said.

'She's at college, but she'll be back later. Do you want me to tell her?'

'Please, Billy Fleming needs his son watched while he cuts Granny's grass.'

'I know him. So what's the deal?'

'I was going to see what Dianne wanted.'

'Leave it to me, although can I ask you a favour?'

'What sort?'

'Nothing bad, it's part of your job. I just wondered if you could talk to her.'

'What about?'

'Just your usual talk to young women about not getting pregnant.'

'Has she got a boyfriend?'

'Not yet, but she's been mooning over Ed Cairns, luckily he's too busy studying.'

'Okay Mrs Dowding, I'll speak to her.'

'Thank you.'

Alice messaged Dianne asking when she'd be back from College before spending the morning running the mother and baby clinic in the surgery. The village wasn't large, and there were few visitors. Shortly before the clinic finished Dianne replied that she was home. Paperwork complete, Alice went over the road to see Dianne.

'Hi Alice, what can I do for you?' said Dianne.

'Didn't your mum say anything?' asked Alice.

'No, she's out, no idea where.'

'Oh, not to worry. I wanted to ask if you minded doing some baby-sitting?'

'Who for?'

'Billy Fleming's little boy. Billy's going to help Granny Jack with her garden.'

'I don't know him, how old is the boy?'

'Billy's the Scottish guy on Stuart Street. The boy has just turned four, he'll be going to school after the summer.'

'Oh, him. I think my Mum knows him.'

'While we're on the subject of your mum, I promised to mention contraception.'

'Will she never stop! I've told her already I'm on the pill, have been since I was 14 just to keep things regular.'

'Well it's only natural she'd worry. How are things going with Ed, by the way?'

'Ed, he's a funny one, terribly clever, but you could hit him with a clue stick the size of a bus and he wouldn't notice.'

'I'm sure he'll notice eventually.'

'Ah! You could help. I'll baby-sit if you get me a date with Ed, and twenty quid to help pay for it a bit.'

'A date and twenty quid? That's asking a lot.'

'What about a date and a tenner then?'

'I can't promise a date.'

'Sure you can, you could use your magic to persuade him.'

'I should think Ed is pretty resistant if you haven't managed it.'

'You can be pretty persuasive when you try.'

'As can you. I'll see what I can do.'

Ed was a tougher nut to crack. He was dedicated to studying and was working flat out on getting good results to make sure he'd get the place he wanted at Cambridge.

Alice knew she'd find Ed in the library, he was there all the hours that it was open. It was right on the outskirts of the village, shared with Upper Harwood, and a stiff 15 minute walk from where she was now.

The library was late Victorian. Over the doors the words 'PUBLIC LIBRARY' were carved deeply. Inside the shelves and furniture were oak, dark with age. Ed was in the corner with the computers, although using his own laptop. Strewn around him were textbooks, papers and a stack of coloured index cards, post-its and pens.

Alice sat on the seat next to Ed, avoiding the abandoned rucksack on the floor. 'Hello Ed, how are you?' she asked. There was no reply, Ed had his earphones jammed in his ears. Alice waved her hand in front of him to get his attention.

'Busy.' he said.

'Don't worry, I came to offer you some help.' Alice said.

'Leave me to get on with it please.'

'Actually I've been reading some research and apparently we learn better when we do it in shorter bursts.'

'Really?'

'Really.' Alice said. 'In fact taking time out to have fun improves your concentration. The longer you study the less effective you become. I can send you the research papers if you like?'

'So why seek me out and tell me this?'

'I know how much you want to get out of here, and I'm a nice person.'

'Oh, really?'

'Well OK, my motive is less pure, but the research is real. I think you'd enjoy the diversion a lot. Not to mention the boost it would give to your studying power.'

'Cite please.'

'Here and now?'

'If you have it?'

'Call up the library catalogue and search if you don't believe me. It's about the effectiveness of overtime rather than studying, but the results hold true.'

Ed brought the laptop closer and searched. Alice watched as he read the abstract.

'OK, close enough. What did you have in mind?' Ed said.

'You know Dianne Dowding?'

'Yeah, she dropped out of school last summer?'

'She's my friend's sister.'

'What about her?'

'Do you like her?' Alice asked. Ed blushed and looked around the library. 'I'll take that as a yes.' Ed nodded. 'Would you like to take her out on a date?'

'Eh?'

'You know, just the two of you, somewhere nice?'

'Oh, yes, of course.'

'Excellent! Where do you want to take her?'

'I've no idea. I've never taken a girl on a date before, what am I supposed to do? Do I need to pay for everything?'

'Why don't you take her to the pictures, I can give you a lift, but you might want to find another way back. Friday night any good?'

'Great, I need to do some research.'

'Does Dianne have your number? Do you want hers?'

'Already got them. Thanks.' Ed was back on his computer looking up advice on taking teenage girls on dates. Alice quietly slipped away.

Having broken Ed, Alice went back to Granny Jack before visiting Fiona. She needed to know how to keep her friend safe, and Granny Jack knew how. Alice gave the door her distinctive knock, the aroma of fresh baked scones met her as she opened the door. Granny was sitting by the fire, knitting.

'Back already dear?' said Granny, 'Why don't you sit down.' she indicated the other chair. The side table next to it featuring a floral china cup and saucer with gently steaming tea, a fruit scone and a small pot of butter.

'Thank you, Granny.' Alice said, taking in the tea and scone ready for her.

'You wanted to ask me about Fiona, didn't you?'

'Yes, I'm really worried about her.'

'And well you might.'

'Granny, you were there, what happened to her mum?'

'No, dear, I wasn't there, that's what happened to her mum, and her granny too. Saved her Aunt though.'

'I thought you were the midwife that delivered her?'

'It was supposed to be me, but someone decided that I had retired and was out of touch. I only found out when it was too late. So yes, I delivered Fiona, but I could have saved her mum if I'd been called earlier.'

'What happened?'

'Gena's waters broke as she was getting out of bed. Her husband called the surgery and they sent round the midwife.'

'Who was that?' Alice asked.

'No-one you'd know, she was new then and didn't stay after what happened.'

'Sorry, carry on please.'

'Well nothing much happened all morning and the midwife went away, telling Gena to phone immediately if her contractions quickened. Well, things happened very quickly at teatime, too quickly. Gena got very rapid strong contractions, and she had a panic attack. Her husband called the midwife, but the surgery was closed. So he called an ambulance. The neighbours heard the commotion, Gena was screaming like her lungs were on fire. They sent someone to get me.

'I arrived before the ambulance could, they were in Stuart Street at the time, and I ran. I ran because I'd been there when Gena's mum had gone and I didn't want that again. It was already too late when I got there though.' Granny stared at the fire.

'You said it was already too late?' Alice said.

'Aye. Gena, god bless her, was still panting and pushing, but nothing was happening. It was all uncoordinated, the body was doing the work, but her mind had moved on. There was no sense being made when you spoke to her.

She was hot to the touch, and her pulse was racing dangerously. I dare say her blood pressure was high too, but I didn't stop to take it. I got on with getting the baby out, because I knew that if I didn't then the baby would go too.'

'So what could you have done if you had been there earlier?'

'If I'd been there I could've kept her calm, that would've helped. But I think that there are other things that might have worked too, not least some of the old remedies.'

'Care to tell me?'

'No, dear, I'll show you. Call me when your friend Fiona is in labour and we'll deliver her together. It's time I passed on some tricks, and I'll not let another Harwood woman die in childbirth.'

Commentary

I outlined three stories, drafted two, and posted one to the TGF. A fourth was outlined and drafted 'First Refusal' before finally writing 'Rounds'. I learnt a lot about planning stories for a specific word count, and practised using many techniques in the course textbook. I also gave and received feedback on drafts.

Creating Characters

I used all four methods of creating characters, one was autobiographical (the Immigration Officer in 'First Refusal'), several were biographical (e.g. Melissa in 'First Refusal' based on several real people drawn from my notebook). Some were pure invention (most characters in 'Rounds') and a few were a combination (e.g. Ed combines invention with me at 17; Granny Jack combines my Granny with the invention of her being a midwife/'wise woman').

For Alice, the primary character in 'Rounds', I drew part of her from the exercises in the second online tutorial and expanded her using exercise 5.1 (Anderson,2006) in reverse. This fleshed out what sort of things she owned, and where she lived. I did something similar for Ed, which was used in the library scene.

Settings

In 'Rounds' there needed to be a number of closely linked scenes to give the impression of a small village with a strong community spirit. This allowed the introduction of several characters and multiple obstacles to create conflict.

I based the physical descriptions on the village I grew up in, although re-arranged to fit narrative requirements. I deliberately left out travel other than as a frame between the scenes. Only just enough detail was included to give the sense of a real place. The focus was on character interaction.

Conflict

An important part of a good story is the equation *'character + conflict = plot'* (Anderson, 2006) so when outlining stories I took care to ensure that there was conflict built in to the structure. I followed my notebook approach in this. This was most marked with 'Rounds' because I decided to put multiple obstacles in the way as part of the story structure.

I tried something similar with 'First Refusal' but this wasn't quite as successful, I think because the flow of the situation didn't allow for the small triumphs to then be replaced with a new obstacle.

Point of View

I also spent some time considering the narrator as discussed in Chapters 7 (first person) & 8 (third person). I considered multiple first person viewpoints, but the word count constraint made this impractical.

I had feedback that changing point of view too often can be confusing. As my TMA01 was written in first person present tense I decided to opt for a third person narrator. I stuck to limited omniscience because the story outlined didn't require information about other events.

Show vs Tell

I determined to show as much as possible and use tell sparingly. The story needed to use dialogue and action with emotion shown from the spoken words, or the actions of characters (Browne & King, 2004).

6 - More on fiction

Meeting the Bechdel Test
18 November 2014

I first came across the Bechdel Test on Charles Stross's blog when he was discussing its importance for pushing gender equality in fiction. . Since becoming aware of the Bechdel test I have consciously tried to meet the spirit of it in all the stuff I write, and as much as I can the actual conditions too.

The Bechdel Test
There are three rules to the test:

1. There are at least two named female characters in the story
2. The women have a conversation
3. The conversation should not be about a man

The Spirit of the Bechdel Test
What I think is most important is meeting the spirit of the test, which as I understand is that **there should be real characters of both genders that aren't just there to be the love interest of another character**.

This is something well worth doing, not only does it promote gender equality (and you could also work in colour and other points of discrimination) but it also makes for more interesting characters that have real differences from each other.

Problem Areas

The most problematical situations are where you have **first person narration by a male character.**

It is almost impossible to easily meet the criteria, the best you can hope for is a three way conversation but even that is problematical because you really need to write it with the male narrator watching rather than participating.

A solution could be switching POV characters between male and female. This works best in longer stories where the split point of view doesn't disrupt the flow.

Short stories are also hard, especially the very short. Even with a female protagonist/POV it can sometimes be difficult (e.g. in a single scene two character piece).

How have I done?

In no particular order, here are some of my pieces of fiction (not all of which have been published) and how they meet the rules and the spirit of the Bechdel Test.

Perfects

The first draft of this near future novel meets all three of the tests, there is a female protagonist (Pandora) and two female supporting characters (Cat & Rosie).

It uses switching POV alternating between a male character and Pandora. In its current iteration Pandora has the larger role of the two and she can properly be shown as the main character.

There are several scenes where Pandora has conversations with one or more of the other female characters, only one of which is about a man.

You can read some excerpts on my blog and tell me in the comments if you think this meets both the letter and the spirit of the Bechdel Test. Scene 08 – Plans being an example of this. **PASS**

Crisis Point
This one is a clear fail in its current version, it is a single character POV. There is only one named female character and she doesn't get to have a conversation with any other female. Certainly none of the conversations are about men, its a military SciFi story.

I certainly could write it with a better gender mix which would help. It is one of the first things I published and pre-dates my knowledge of the test, and also my creative writing course. I do want to re-write it and publish an updated version that would work better. **FAIL**

Planting the Past
Planting the Past (see above) is short piece I wrote early in my creative writing course. It has a female POV and the only two characters in it are a husband and wife.

So it fails on that score. This story isn't really long enough to be capable of re-writing to meet the criteria, it's not really a whole story just a single scene.

Perhaps if it was expanded more could be done. I could almost see it as the opening scene of a longer work, and it did inspire Hunting Nazis (see below). **FAIL**

Hunting Nazis

Hunting Nazis is the story I wrote for the end of module assessment, it is included later in this volume and hasn't been previously published. It is a sort of urban fantasy/horror told from a female POV.

It is sort of X-Files meets the SOE, Dot was an SOE agent in WW2 and she has teamed up with Reggie (the husband and wife from Planting the Past) and they are tying up loose ends of Nazi occultism from the war.

This piece is set in a Berlin club and some nearby bunkers. I managed to squeeze in a couple of other female characters and a conversation in the toilets trying to gather information.

It is a bare pass though (I was pushed for word count, and this bit was heavily trimmed). **PASS**

Rounds

Rounds was my piece for the fiction assignment on A215. It features a female protagonist and she has several conversations with other characters in the course of the story, the named characters are three female to two male and the conversations are 4-2 in favour of the women.

None of the conversations is about men (although one of the conversations does involve brokering a date in return for a favour). I'd certainly rate this is a good pass, especially since I deliberately wrote it to pass the Bechdel test (as well as the assignment criteria). **PASS**

Razor Blade

An unpublished (and not quite finished) military science fiction piece set several hundred years in the future. The main character is a female naval officer and the named characters are an even mix of genders.

There is at least one conversation in the current draft between her and her Aunt (a senior political figure in the Admiralty) about a special mission that most definitely isn't about a man.

When finished it will be a really easy pass as half of the conversations in it will feature at least two women, and it isn't going to feature them worrying about men!
PASS

Daprav

Daprav is really the name of the state in a fantasy world where I ran a D&D campaign a decade ago. However I have started to write a story based on the campaign.

The characters come from the players, who were a mixed bunch of students mostly, with a couple of older guys helping it along (me being one of them, I was 29 which is ancient in undergraduate terms). Three out of the seven primary character group are female, and like Perfects it uses switching POV.

This means that there is plenty of scope for it passing the Bechdel Test. As planned it will do exactly that, however I've not yet written the dialogue in any of the scenes where female characters have conversations (but they do have an outline showing what the scene is about, and most of them feature discussions about things other than men). **PASS**

Dialogue: Five Facts for Fantastic Dialogue
17 August 2015

Dialogue can be difficult, but there are some things you can do to make it way better. Here are five things for you to focus on when editing your dialogue. If you do these then your dialogue will be amazing. As with everything, you need make sure the dialogue advances the plot or develops the characters. If it doesn't do either, or both, then cut it out.

Dialogue Directions

1. Read it out loud

2. *Show* the emotions

3. Give each character their own voice

4. Use only 'said'

5. Keep it short

Read it Out Loud

This is how you know that you've got the rhythm right. If you can, record yourself reading it and listen back. Don't take any shortcuts. You need to actually say it out loud, reading in your head doesn't work. This is good advice for all of your text, but does double duty for dialogue.

Show the Emotions

Good dialogue tells the reader what the character is feeling. Never use attributions to do that. Sometimes though the dialogue itself isn't enough for this.

So show some of the body language through bits of character action as well.

For example, compare

'Yes!' He shouted excitedly.

'Yes!' He pumped his fist.

The dialogue is the same, but in the second example you've shown the emotion with the fist pump rather than telling it with an attribution.

Unique voices

All your characters are different. So make them sound different. Think about them and what they have as interests, their level of education and social background.

All of these colour what people talk about and the words they choose. This should come out in the dialogue that you write for them.

The way to test it is when you are reading aloud. If you can tell which character is speaking from the dialogue then you've got it about right. The true test is when other people can do that.

Only use 'said'

One of the things that's really easy to do with first drafts is to get into lazy attributions. You just want to bash the story out and being a proper writer you resist the urge to edit as you do it. This leads to he argued, she said languidly and other similar things.

If you've been showing the emotion properly then these crutches don't add anything and so they need to be removed.

In fact you should lose any attributions you can and the rest should only be 'character said'. The sole purpose of a dialogue attribution is to make it clear who is speaking.

If there are only two characters involved in a back and forth, and you've given them both their own distinctive voice, then you can largely dispense with the attributions.

Keep it short

Dialogue works best with a series of short bursts. When you listen to people speak, it is rare for one person to make a Shakespeare style soliloquy. Also you want to break up text with whitespace to make the dialogue easier to read.

Start each new speaker on their own line, and break if anyone else does anything or you need to switch out of dialogue. This keeps it short.

Cell Tradecraft – Plot Hole Plugged
28 August 2015

The cell tradecraft in the first draft of Perfects had a plot hole. I found in my first editing pass, it relates to what the cell does when it is compromised.

Background
The main characters in Perfects are a group of genetically modified people. They're illegal and trying to help other genetically modified people escape from the country under false identities.

The parallel here is the evader networks in nazi occupied Europe during WW2. Indeed the group has consciously modelled it's way of working on the SOE manual. They have a compartmentalised cell structure to prevent the whole network being compromised.

The Plot Hole
The story involves the cell being compromised. The police raid their identity factory and arrest of a couple of the cell members, including the leader.

In the first draft as written I had them following a pre agreed plan to make their escape from the area. This makes sense from the perspective that the extraction plan is thought through. Also that there is pre positioned escape kit to facilitate this.

However, it doesn't work from an operational security perspective. If the police break the first person before you've got out of the country, then they can pick everyone else up. So this hole needed to be fixed.

SOE worked on the basis that everyone will break under interrogation, and that double agents will infiltrate your network.

So you limit who knows what as much as possible. You also change things frequently so that it is harder for anyone to spot a pattern. Most of these lessons were learnt the hard way.

So the cell needs to assume that it will be betrayed. This most likely what lead to their identity workshop being raided. Their early warning system saved them from being caught in the act, although the police operation still picked up two of them nearby.

Cell Tradecraft – Actions On Compromise

The fix is simple. The cell should have a set of actions on compromise already worked out.

1. None of the cell know all of the options for the escape plan.
2. The cell will have multiple escape plans.
3. Every cell member has at least one false identity and hideout that no one else knows about
4. Every cell member has private contact arrangements 1:1 with every other cell member.

So the drill on finding out about a potential cell compromise is to scatter and lie low using 3 until it is clear whether or not the cell has been compromised. When it has been compromised then the cell members can gather using the arrangements at 4 if that seems sensible. If not then each cell member can invoke their private extraction plan.

Any cell member that the police have had arrested needs to be treated as suspect and told nothing. Ideally not even contacted to avoid the risk that they've been turned.

7 - World Building

Compelling fiction needs to be set in a credible world. Contemporary fiction gets round this by using the real world as it is, with only minor differences to support the plot. When writing other genres the author needs to build their own worlds. Even if you are very well versed in stringing words together, if the reader cannot believe the story you are weaving, then it will fall flat.

Five Reasons for Establishing a Colony
19 November 2013

In looking through my notes from previous story and game design ideas I came across one about the reasons why colonies might be set up. This was primarily for a set of scenarios for science fiction games that a group of us having been playing around the Full Moon each month since 1996.

That said, they are based on actual historical reasons why people left the UK and other European countries to live elsewhere (although not always on an uncertain and dangerous frontier).

1. Religious/Ascetic Freedom

This covers people leaving to avoid discrimination as well as those that might want to live in a place where the temptations and 'polluting influences' of modern life are not present.

Examples of this include Amish and similar sects that avoid advanced technology (although quite why they'd get in a spaceship I'm not sure). Features of this sort of colony may include:

- lack of high-tech industry (unless necessary to sustain the colony – even them imports would be more likely);
- Colonists will be complete family groups, from birth to death;
- no luxury housing or flashy entertainment (forget the five star hotel complex or New Vegas);
- primarily farming, fishing and hunting;
- minimal mining & raw materials processing (mainly for construction and export);
- very tight group, outsiders would be obvious and shunned if not co-religionists. There may be restricted areas only for the faithful if there are frequent visits by groups not sharing similar beliefs;
- no significant police/security apparatus, discipline would be enforced by social norms and religious leaders;
- Outside support may be a necessary requirement to maintain the colony;
- Only co-religionists would be accepted for settlement.

2. Mining Colony

In a place where surveys have shown significant concentrations of valuable minerals then there may be an attempt to settle on a commercial basis.

This is the equivalent of the oil rig workers in remote parts of Earth, or perhaps the mid-19th century California or Australian pioneers looking for gold. Features of this sort of colony could include;

- everyone on the colony is employed by, or contracted to, a specific company or consortium;
- Colonists are likely to be single adults of working age without dependents;
- heavily geared around mineral extraction and perhaps also processingl;
- they could be focussed on producing stuff for export, and also on individuals returning home again when they've completed their tour, or struck it rich;
- minimal manufacturing, agriculture or any construction not required for the mining and export operations;
- limited off-world support, if not profitable within a short time period the colony will be closed down again and all colonists repatriated;
- small security capability, mainly geared around dealing with drunk & bored miners on an off-duty binge (i.e. a security team rather than a police force, discipline is company and offenders are likely to have pay docked or be sent home as sanctions).

3. Farming/Ranching

This one is perhaps more an outcome of a collection of other motivations, but perhaps also from people that can't get the space to have their own farm in the home country, and instead choose to emigrate in the hope of getting their own land.

Certainly this seems to have been a common enough motivation for some of the 18th & early 19th century settlers in North America. Features of this sort of colony may include:

- lots of agriculture, and strong exports of food and other agricultural products (especially luxury products);
- Colonists will be heavily weighted to adults of working age, but will also include family groups, although perhaps few elderly in the early stages;
- lots of small settlements, spaced reasonably far apart, perhaps 10-20kms from each other with cultivated land between them;
- limited mining and heavy industry, and what is there will be geared to supporting the agricultural industry;
- well developed chemical and pharmaceutical industries, as well as food and materials processing to turn produce into saleable goods that are worth more as exports;
- Neglible police/security (think more one man sherrif/constable alongside his farming/other duties with backup from the posse if required).

4. A Better Life[TM]

Isn't this really the motivation for everyone that decides to get up from where they are and go somewhere else?

The typical example here is probably the current migrations of people to other countries. This sort of thing is less likely to directly establish a colony, but is probably a pretty common second wave that could make the difference between a colony bumping along at subsistence level and really making it. Features of a colony with a high proportion of better lifers might include:

- mature long established colony (perhaps at least 5-10 years old);
- lots of recent arrivals, with a broad population mix (including babies and children, but not many elderly until the colony is well established);
- an above average economy with high living standards (luxury housing, entertainment, range of consumer goods and agricultural produce);
- a work hard, play hard culture (immigrants tend to be harder working, and they have a determination to succeed – regardless of what you might have read in the Daily Fail);
- high productivity leading to sustainable living at better than subsistence level;
- likely use of robots, automation and other high tech industries within a broad economic base;
- Mature police and justice system, as a consequence of maturity of the colony with a sustained population growth.

5. Political/Doctrinal Dissidents

There will be loads of different political systems and doctrinal variations that will lead to people choosing to leave. Some of these may co-exist on the same continent/planet as fallings out happen and it is expensive to relocate further awayt. Others may be new colonies that are settled from a homeland.

Historical examples of this include the Jacobites that moved to Canada in the 18th Century, or perhaps some of the dissidents from Eastern Europe that made their home in London in the nineteenth. There may also be examples of small towns in North America settled this way too. Some features of these colonies may include:

- some oddly extreme governance models;

- mostly adults of working age, perhaps towards the younger end of this (I've noticed that people tend to soften in their political activism with age). Total population is likely to be relatively modest, and may be kept that way by frequent splits;

- unless the political/doctrinal belief prohibits it, there will be a lot of automation and robots in use to run the economy (after all there isn't time for a good political argument if you need to work very hard all day to make ends meet);

- the economy is likely to be based on a few things and be relatively spartan (from necessity rather than for doctrinal reasons);

- strong police/security environment. This may not be immediately obvious, but there is a close relationship between extremism and strict enforcement of thought typical of police states.

Economics of New Colonies

I often try to write hard SF stories. I've been thinking about how new colonies get set up and the sort of funding they need.

There is a lot of infrastructure required to build a viable colony on a new system. Firstly you need to survey it to find a good spot with a reasonable confluence of resources, mining sites, farming space, fresh water, building land and a suitable area for your drop zone and spaceport.

Once you've done that some cheap housing, utilities, early resource processing plants and factories for essentials have to be built. Once you get to that point you might just start exporting valuable things, although you'll still need to import lots of essentials, not to mention more people.

I reckon that it is a minimum of two years to get to the point where the exports cover the costs of the imports. At that point the colony investors are probably starting to think about seeing a return on their investment. Using the macro campaign rules as a guide a two year subsistence colony has probably racked up about 200 million credits in debt.

The tax take of local government is no more that enough to service the interest and provide some basic leadership and policing. The overall economy of the colony is probably only a little bigger than the debt, perhaps 300 million credits a year. There are probably about 150,000 colonists on the planet (maybe more if there are many dependents with the workers).

So in the normal course of things one would expect the economy to grow with migration and in due course the extra tax revenue would pay back the capital and also provide the additional services that the colony's people required.

There may even be pump priming investment in infrastructure to keep things moving. That said, the people might not come, or the government could make poor decisions, or there could be some natural disaster.

If the colony collapses what happens then? In total failures the banks / investors will just need to write off the debt, while perhaps keeping a nominal ownership of the assets left behind in case a subsequent colonisation effort wants to take over.

There might not be a total failure, in which case a restructuring of debt would be required. Although depending on the reasons there might be difficulty getting more money.

Another thing that could happen is a conflict with another colony in the same planet, especially when colonies on better developed planets realise that they would be better off as a large single entity in gaining access to trade agreements with other interstellar groups.

What happens to state debt when another state takes it over?

In the case of a hostile takeover (either a war or a share buyout) there will be an expectation that the structural debt will be taken on by the new management. The banks will insist on this, and if the new management doesn't agree then they will treat it the same was as defaulting on the loan payments.

Refusing to make payments against a loan has serious consequences and it is to be avoided. If times are difficult it is expected that the colony management will talk to the banks and/or investors to either extend the payback time or raise sufficient funds through other means to ensure that they continue to properly service debt in an agreed fashion.

Any colony that defaults can expect the following to happen:

- no further lines of credit will be opened, so all capital expenditure will need to be paid for up front, also future interest rates will be higher to represent the increased risk of default
- imports may not be possible, except perhaps at black market rates for items
- prices on exports may be lower than expected (and indeed cargoes may be seized in lieu of debt interest and/or capital)
- Enforcement action may be taken to seize colonial assets, especially movable ones (although a colony with strong armed forces may find this won't happen)

- Other colonies in the same system may come under pressure not to co-operate, similarly trade agreements may be suspended or even revoked.
- In extreme cases an interim management may be installed, possibly by a major polity if the colony is sufficiently well off to have attracted attention.
- Immigration is likely to slow down, and colonists are more likely to leave the colony

Towns and Villages
26 December 2014

One of the things that I often do when I am writing a story is to sketch a map of the area where the story takes place. This helps me to visualise what the characters will be able to see.

The thing is though, you can't just bang down stuff randomly (well you can, but it isn't realistic – you do want your world to be realistic don't you?)

How settlements form
Typically people build houses where there is shelter from the elements, adequate supplies of food, water and fuel.

They also like to build them in easily accessible places for the most part. All villages and towns grow from farmstead, places a farmer, and his family, decided to settle.

However not all of these farmsteads ends up as a village. There are loads of outlying farms in populated countryside, some of them are ancient or at least built on the remains of an ancient farm. What distinguishes those that get bigger?

There's an element of luck, but mainly it is because they either have an abundance of some resource or they lie along a convenient route.

Trade is the reason most of our towns exist. Certainly this is true of the most ancient ones. There are exceptions to this, but these tend to be modern capital cities (Washington DC being an example) or new towns intended to displace people from densely populated inner cities (like Milton Keynes, or Cumbernauld).

Villages

Look closely at the next handful of villages you drive through. There is a clear difference between an extended farm with houses for the labourers and a proper village. *Villages tend to have a focal point*, usually a green space, but sometimes a market square. Modern villages still have them, there will be an open area possibly with a children's play area.

Around this there will be a Church, possibly a pub, a shop or two and often a war memorial. Even if there isn't an open area there will be a cluster of the Church (with graveyard), a pub, shop and war memorial. These will be surrounded with houses, perhaps along a single linear road.

If there is a second cross road this may also have houses along it. The cross roads (sometimes a Y) will often run on two sides of the Church, or the village green if there is one. Optional extras, depending on the size of the village

- village hall (1,000 residents to be viable);

- school (needs a couple of hundred kids aged 4-11 within five miles to work);

- more shops and pub (scale up shops per 200 inhabitants, and pubs per thousand);

- larger villages have more streets, keeping everything within minimum walking distance.

Of course when you are world building for a story you **make the village suit the narrative** that you are conveying. It doesn't really matter if the shops, pubs or anything else is economically viable.

If you need an internal rivalry then two pubs might be a way to do it. If you need a football team, or a Women's Institute then write in the Pavilion and pitch, or the village hall or whatever you need.

Communities

A key feature of villages is that **typically people know their neighbours**, and in the smaller more settled ones far outside the commuter belt, the lineages of all the residents. Or at least some of the inhabitants know all of that. This can be a feature for interesting stories.

The other thing that happens in these sorts of communities is that the smarter kids leave for university and jobs in the big city. Some of the others join the services (including some of the smart ones) and go away that way.

Often they reappear later in life, retired in their forties, or professionally qualified as the local GP, district nurse, solicitor, entrepreneur, mechanic. This is a good way to bring people in later on without having to make them complete strangers to the rest of your characters.

Towns

Towns are a whole different order of magnitude different. They don't scale into villages, there is a sort of multiplier effect with proper towns. Almost every old town that I have looked at, and I do pay attention on my travels, is based around a market, and very often also a river crossing.

Towns tend to be on the nexus of trade routes, and they draw in people from surrounding villages for markets and also specialised trades. As well as being bigger than villages, especially with the tradespeople, they also have a lot more in the way of amenities.

There will be a square, with a town hall of some sort on it, and often also a church. In many modern towns the square has been infilled, usually with parades of shops, descended from the market stalls that once stood in the same place.

Like the villages the towns are often formed around a crossroads, this can be two sides of the main square, or sometimes they join at one end of a widened high street and then split out after the shopping area (Reigate in Surrey does this, the A25 and A217 being the primary routes).

Another key feature of a town, other than being astride a trade route, is that it tends to have an abundance of something useful (or it did have in its early days). This could be something simple like weavers in a sheep farming region, or a watermill in an arable area.

There ought to be something. This might not matter to your story though and you don't need to worry about it much. However it could also be useful as a hook, or a clue.

How I draw maps

Firstly I think of the sort of place that I need for my story, and the key locations I need it to have. Once I've listed those out I get myself a blank sheet of paper (although I do sometimes use squared paper).

I draw using a 2B pencil, this lets me rub bits out and move them if I need to. I usually start with some outline topographical features (which way is uphill, where are the water courses).

Then I put the focus of the village/town on the map, along with some routes. I see this as growing the town organically.

Next down are the key locations I need relative to each other. I then fill in the gaps between them with the other necessary parts of the village/town. i.e. the pubs, shops and civic amenities. If it is a mediaeval walled town then I add these in now as well. If there is a need for industry I also stick that in too.

Lastly I add in some houses for the people to live in, making sure to put the bigger ones upwind of the town (the richer districts of towns/cities tend to be upwind on prevailing winds because the rich folk can afford to build where the air is sweeter).

I try to put in at least one building for every ten inhabitants, in modern times maybe two to three times that much, we live much less densely these days, even though there are more of us.

When I'm happy with the overall shape then I ink in the important bits and use colour (following the UK ordnance survey colour scheme for the most part). This just makes the map a little bit faster to read.

Mid 21st Century Policing
17 June 2015

I've been thinking about how policing in the UK might evolve over the next few decades. This is a combination of evaluating the background I've done for Perfects and also looking at perhaps running some more near future police roleplaying over the summer. I'm going to pick an arbitrary date of 2040, 25 years in the future.

One thing I'm sure won't change is the concept of policing by consent. It's a fundamental plank of how we do things in Britain, and we know that it works. Other things that I think are given are

- budget pressures (the perennial urging to do more with less)
- the adoption of new technology to transform how policing happens
- visible policing with people on the ground

So it's an evolution of traditional policing rather than a pivot to Judge Dredd, the latter definitely isn't a by consent style of policing. The change is akin to the transformation of policing from the 1970s until now. The time frame is slightly shorter although one can fairly safely argue that police reform was kickstarted by the 1984 Police and Criminal Evidence Act (PACE).

As William Gibson is noted for observing:

"the future is already here,
it's just unevenly distributed"

We can see the beginnings of a number of things in the way police use technology

- police in Hampshire have been wearing cameras for a few years
- police in Merseyside had a drone (until it crash landed in the Mersey)
- police helicopters are used to track escaping people and vehicles to vector police officers to arrest them
- Automatic Number Plate Recognition (ANPR) cameras are now standard in police vehicles. Linked to a mobile data terminal they let police know who owns the vehicle, if it is taxed and insured etc.
- Facial recognition / matching has a wide range of applications including the automated gates at the Border control.

So there are a wide range of technologies that are currently being proven and are likely to be adopted across police services. Budget cuts and imperatives from the centre to cooperate more will drive uptake.

What we are likely to see is a greater homogenisation of the police services, perhaps with some mergers.

Police are very likely to be wearing cameras well before 2040. They'll likely be required by law to record their interactions with you. In the early days of this it will no doubt lose some police officers their jobs, but the police will get used to it and in due course it will increase confidence in their impartiality and honesty.

People will find ways around this but I would expect the video will be streamed to a secure server where individual officers weren't able to tamper with it.

Another key feature is ANPR for people. Police will use biometric capture from their cameras to identify people. I'd expect beat police to have some sort of head up display that indicated interesting people to them.

This will save a lot of police time in trying to identify people. It might also change some of the criminal attitudes to things too. Getting caught is a side effect of the career for them, they might wriggle less on identity in future and look for other ways of denying wrongdoing.

Drones won't replace officers on the street but they might replace most of the helicopters, and bring more overhead surveillance into play.

Current UAV technology is pretty flaky, there are a lot of crashes, but it will improve. I can see a range of uses and sizes for drones.

One particular one that might appear over busy crowds is a chaser. Small with 360 degree cameras, a speaker and a taser it could track a fleeing suspect through a crowd where a human would lose them.

It would need to be small enough to fly through doorways etc. The speaker is for warning the suspect to stop and await arrest. The taser is backup if the speaker doesn't do the trick.

More on 21st Century Policing
24 June 2015

Last week I wrote about some general trends in the future of policing and touched a little on the use of drones to help enforcement and make it easier for the police to catch fleeing criminals. This week I'm going to look at some of the personal kit that police officers are likely to come equipped with as standard.

First some key assumptions

- stupid criminals will still try to stab/shoot/injure police officers, so armour is here to stay
- British policing by consent will require our police to have faces, to interact with the public and to walk the beat in busy public places
- Regulations on evidence will remain, possibly updated in light of new technology and possibilities (although the fact that PACE has lasted thirty years without calls to change it suggest that it is a pretty good piece of legislation)
- Budget cuts, and the key political metric of 'Bobbies on the Beat', will lead to streamlining paperwork to get as many of the PCs out of the station as possible (perhaps with smaller office footprints to save money).

Again, taking the William Gibson view, we have the following extant or experimental technologies that might help the police transform their efficiency levels without compromising public protection.

- google glass, or something similar allowing head up displays as well as recording of events
- police radios already support mesh networking, data transmission and are issued on an individual basis
- firearms are starting to get chip controls to limit who can use them (see Judge Dredd) and the US government is working on linking this to tactical HUD for soldiers, so police firearms officers could get this too
- eye control is being worked on, currently paraplegics and fast jet fighter pilots are getting it, but given time it will be available more widely
- data analytics is starting to get very good and approaching real time, linking the data out of the PNC into a HUD along with other publicly or government information will be possible
- voice to text and voice recognition software is improving steadily.
- smartphones are ubiquitous and people tend to take them everywhere and keep them switched on
- CCTV cameras aren't going to disappear

So this gives an ordinary police officer that looks remarkably like one you might see today, but with wraparound see through glasses with elements of a Head Up Display (HUD) to help them identify people and tag anyone they'd like to follow or speak with.

If this is linked back to the PNC info and some facial matching then you get the ability to identify most of the population very rapidly and to understand their assurance rating. Potentially known offenders can be flagged, especially if they have violent tendencies or are wanted in connection with a crime.

There's also the ability to bring back other relevant records, medical where people have conditions that could be aggravated by stress or confinement (this needs some care, you wouldn't automatically show everything about anyone to a police officer, there'd need to be some proportionality to it and it would need to be relevant to an enquiry).

This would make police officers more effective, especially detectives. Where they needed to talk to people they can start off knowing the answers to the identity questions, giving them more leverage with the unco-operative.

It would also make life easier because the paperwork wouldn't need to be done later, it could be done while an interview was in progress with good speech to text for transcripts, semantic tagging of the video using eye control and perhaps even a built in stress/lie detector.

If this was also combined with an ability to access location based use of a smartphone (or whatever replaces smartphones) on a suspect, probably with direct permission at the time, then it could rapidly exclude lots of people from enquiries when combined with the CCTV records.

This wouldn't stop crime, it would change the patterns of crime and force the career and organised criminals to be a lot more professional in what they do to avoid being caught. It would probably also let the police roll up gangs when one of them made a mistake, as the records linking them together are going to be easier to join with better analytics than they are now.

It can and is done now, but it isn't a real time process yet, it can take weeks of digging by skilled analysts to identify the networks. By 2040 we might have got to where the movies have us now.

Forensics technology is also going to come on leaps and bounds. We've already got to the point where you can make a DNA barcode with a handheld device. This is only going to improve over the next 25 years.

I doubt it will go as far as every police officer being so equipped, forensics is a delicate and specialist role. However what it will do is allow faster results, and perhaps detectives could run DNA profiles during interviews with suspects, which could help eliminate or implicate them faster.

It will also make it a lot harder for criminals to deny that they've been somewhere, although I expect that counter-measures to DNA scanning will start to appear.

Self Driving Cars
1 July 2015

I've written about advances in police technology, but one of the other technology changes that has a major societal impact is self driving cars. People have been talking about this for years, and recently both Google and Elon Musk are seriously working on self driving cars. Other companies are too, but not to the same extent.

Progress Report on Self Driving Cars
Google released a report on where they'd got to with self driving cars. They plan to report monthly. By mid-2015 their self driving cars had clocked up 1.1 million miles in autonomous mode, and been involved in 12 accidents.

None of those accidents were the fault of the self driving cars, in fact for 8 of the 12 the vehicle was stationary. If you ignore the five accidents where the self driving cars were actually under manual control, then they were stationary in 6 out of 7 cases, and the 7th involved a human in another car changing lanes when driving parallel to the self driving car.

What this tells me is that the self driving cars are probably safer on the road than we are. The more milage they clock up, and the lower the rate of accidents they've caused, the easier it will be to argue that they are safer than us.

When that happens then we shall probably start to see them appear in our car showrooms. As well as

California, where they are being tested, the UK has already approved the principle of self driving cars on the roads.

Benefits of Self Driving Cars

Self driving cars will change how we behave as much as they improve road safety. My three year old daughter might never learn to drive, by the time she is old enough it is likely that self driving cars will be common that it won't be worth the time and money to bother learning to control a fully manual vehicle.

If you drive you'll know that where you park your vehicle when you get to your destination is a major factor. With a self-driving car you could just step out at the nearest place that you can stop and get on with what you came for. The car will then drive off and park itself somewhere and come back when you call it.

The self driving cars will be networked, so they'll know where the spaces are, and they can pack in more closely than humans can, especially if you don't need to worry about opening the doors.

The other feature of networked self driving cars is that they can co-ordinate while moving to keep the traffic flowing. This should smooth out a lot of the stop start that you get on motorways when someone brakes a little too enthusiastically and the car behind a little more. Ten miles back traffic comes to a complete halt.

This just won't happen. Also if we still have traffic lights, these can be added to the network and be very smart indeed. Most cases the lights wouldn't even need to activate, only if there was a manual driver detected in the flow of traffic.

Manual driving would probably end up like smoking, seen as a dangerous thing but tolerated in its reservations (go to a track if you want to drive a car, but don't endanger others by doing it in company).

Social Impacts of Autonomous Vehicles

Self driving cars are starting to look safer than human drivers and that there are traffic management benefits to most vehicles being self-driving. But there's more to it than that. For a start there will be more than just 'cars' that drive themselves around, so properly one ought to talk about autonomous vehicles (AV).

No More Professional Drivers

The most obvious consequence of autonomous vehicles is that those who drive for a living will rapidly be out of a job. The cost base for taxis, truck haulage and bus companies involves driver pay plus the costs of running and maintaining the vehicle.

I expect that initially there will be an added capital cost for the autonomous version of vehicles, but that will be offset by savings from driver pay, reduced insurance costs (because the AV are safer than the humans) and also increased usage of the vehicle, because in most jurisdictions there are limits on driver hours.

This is not a benefit if you are a driver, but in the same way that other skills have been automated (e.g. robots used to build vehicles) it is inevitable. There may still be humans in some of the vehicles, but they'll be for security or unloading and they won't be paid the same as the professional drivers used to be.

They'll also not really have limits on hours, because mostly they are just passengers. Expect them to be minimum wage jobs, maybe even split shift and only paid when they're loading or unloading.

The current owner/operators of heavy goods vehicles might carve out a niche where they live in the vehicle and deal with the security and unloading as well as managing their business while it cruises the motorways from delivery to delivery. They'd get a lot more mileage in without the driving limits.

Mobile Homes & Commuting
Given the cost of living in major cities there is a niche for a mobile home that cruises between parking areas. So long as it costs you less to maintain and operate than a city centre flat plus the commuting then some single people, and perhaps couples, might live in an autonomous mobile home.

It would know where they need to be and when and would drift towards the destination on a low impact path (low impact in the sense that it would be looking for a steady fuel efficient speed and avoid areas where sudden braking or manoeuvring might be needed).

In the context of London you could orbit via the M25 or the North & South Circular until almost time for being dropped off at an easy walking distance from work. The mobile home would then park itself somewhere (or keep on orbiting) until you signalled that you were on the way back to the pick up point.

If you needed to work in a different location, or had a day off and wanted to be somewhere else it could drive you there while you slept.

The key point here is that your front door would move itself to where you wanted it to be for when you needed it to be there. The AV would do this as fuel efficiently and as safely as possible (and possibly with solar panels all over it to help save fuel costs).

While not likely to be a first option for many people it would solve some affordable housing problems and also make it easier for job seekers to cover larger areas without wasting awake time with commuting. I doubt it would be any good for families, but certainly something that some people might find attractive. There could also be a strong holiday rental aspect to these vehicles.

I expect that fewer people will be commuting overall in a decade or two, but those that do may well go further than drivers do now. Autonomous vehicles potentially make all commutes into public transport type commutes.

You can work, read, watch video or even sleep in transit when someone else (the vehicle) is doing the driving. This can make you more tolerant of time spent in transit, because you are getting productive use from it.

While AV should eventually do away with the traffic jam, because they'll route efficiently to keep everyone moving satisfactorily, before it manages that it will at least take away some of the pain.

Renting Vehicles
There are already schemes to rent vehicles by the hour, or by the day. However they need a fair amount of infrastructure to operate. With an AV fleet you can simply rent the right size of vehicle you need for the journey you want to do and then return it the moment you step out at your destination.

More like Uber than Zipcar. If the pricing is right many people will stop trying to own their own vehicles and just use pooled ones.

Someone will still need to act as a fleet manager, but the costs of maintaining depots and dealing with deliveries and returns go out of the window. With a bit of optimisation a number of small parking areas (likely on street in areas not needing permits) can be used instead of depots.

When ordered the closest available vehicle will make its way to the customer for use. If the routes are booked in advance there will be the possibility of pre-positioning and forward optimisation.

AV might even stay at the last drop off point until they are next needed, on the basis that people tend to go and return on the same route.

There will be a blurring here between how we currently rent cars and how we use taxis. The future model is a hybrid of both of these. It might even blur into how we use busses and trains.

Someone is likely to grab a niche that picks up multiple folk along the way and bill everyone for the appropriate fraction of the journey they consume. It's a startup waiting to happen.

Freedom for non-drivers

Another thing that autonomous vehicles will bring is more freedom for people that cannot drive. Teenagers and older people, as well as those that haven't had the time or the money to invest in driving lessons (not to mention those that are incapable) will be able to get around in AVs, providing that they can afford them.

That said, I expect that the rental costs will be relatively modest twenty or so years down the road, certainly cheaper than a taxi is now (most of the cost is in paying the driver). For the affluent families it will be reasonable to let the almost grown up kids take the car out for the night.

The AV will be safer than they would be now, cheaper to insure and there is no need to pay for expensive driving lessons. For an 18 year old an AV is likely to be their cheapest way to get mobile. Also, there's no worries about drink driving, as the car won't be drinking!

For older folk at the other end of the driving spectrum there should be less worry about capacity to drive when faculties start to dwindle. The car should know where home is, and could even be pre-programmed with an itinerary by a carer or relative.

For those in full possession of their faculties that wouldn't be necessary, but the car can take the strain and ensure that they can get around and enjoy life.

Part 3 – Poetry

8 - Learning about poetry

Poetry – Coffee Cravings
20 January 2014

Having done the section on fiction (and written a 2,200 word short story, or rather four of them, two of which were too long) the next part of the course is on Poetry.

For six weeks I'll be trying to write some poetry. I was finding poetry rather baffling, I've never had a problem writing prose, it just sort of rolls off smoothly.

The first chapter in the Big Red Book about it, Chapter 12, wasn't really helpful for me, I didn't think it offered anything new over what we've already covered at the beginning of the course. Mainly it was a series of writing prompts and exercises on inciting creativity.

There was nothing about what made this stream of text poetry as opposed to prose.

However, Chapter 13 is quite different, and while reading it I've done first drafts of two poems, one of which is my own attempt at exercise 13.5.

The bit that clicked for me was the discussion of poetry as a spoken form rather than written. How there needed to be rhythm, pace and timing in reading it. The discussion on alliteration, rhyme and how the form of poetry changed with the increase in literacy sort of made it make sense for me.

This doesn't mean I'm now a crack poet, but it made me happy enough to give it a go. Just as well really, because I need to manage 40 lines of good quality poetry for TMA03.

Coffee Cravings

Always alert, always awaited.
Beans bringing brightness.

Clasping my caffeinated cup until it cools
drinking until only dregs dirty the mug
each and every day until I effervesce.

Full of body, full of flavour.
Guilt free, give it to me.

I cannot live without coffee

Meta Poetry

30 January 2014

The third online tutorial is now on the go, following a poetry day school last weekend (where I read out some Burns since it was the 25th). Anyway the exercise is to write a poem based on the model of Amanda Dalton's How to Disappear.

So this is the second draft of my meta poem, a further draft (poetry as a process) will be posted later on when I've had some feedback and had time to let it rest a wee bit.

NB – for the poetry the formatting isn't always perfect, especially this one where I have used some long lines. You might want to view the original on the web on a landscape monitor where you can see where the line breaks are intended to go.

http://www.themself.org/2014/01/a215-meta-poetry/

How to write poetry

How can an ordinary person like me possibly do it?
How am I supposed to get all those words arranged on
    the page?
How do I learn to write beautiful poetry?

Recognise that poetry doesn't appear ready to read. Like
    a block of stone,
it needs careful chiselling, chip by chip, into shape. What
    goes is important
as what stays. Ready to restore errant chunks where the
    chisel chips too much.

Read it. Write it. Read it again. Read it out loud.
Read it until I am proud of every word, line
break and punctuation mark. Stop and think
about how structure shapes story, how the line breaks
    change
meaning. Embrace the choice
of word and make every word sweat.

Write it. Shape it. Share it.

What They Teach you at Creative Writing School

1 February 2014

I read this article by Hanif Kureishi about his views on what is missing from the teaching of creative writing http://www.telegraph.co.uk/culture/books/10594606/Hanif-Kureishi-What-they-dont-teach-you-at-creative-writing-school.html.

I don't entirely agree with Hanif Kureishi. Perhaps if he'd studied with the Open University he would have had plenty of practice in recognising the plentiful supply of good ideas that we have. He might also have been taught some techniques to fire up his imagination and to harness it to produce material.

On the other hand I do agree that there is (understandably) a lot of focus in textbooks on the 'hard' skills that writers need. On use of language, structure and the practicalities of how to produce good prose, poetry etc. This is not just down to creative writing schools though, all disciplines have a mixture of 'hard' and 'soft' skills. Generally it is much easier to teach people the 'hard' skills, because you can measure success in applying them so much more easily.

The true masters of any discipline can do both the 'hard' and the 'soft' very well, but it is typically much easier to teach a 'hard' skill than a 'soft' skill.

An example of this is interviewing people. You can readily teach people how to structure an interview, what sort of questions to ask and how to document it all. It is very much harder to teach someone how to tell if the interviewee is credible, and how to make a judgement based on the given answers.

Creative writing is no different, you know the great from the good when you read it. Having the techniques doesn't help you deliver great writing. It is much harder to be certain that what you are writing is as good as it could be. Even when you do your best there is still a level of subjectivity on what is great writing.

The avoidance of that subjectivity is what makes universities (and anyone accrediting performance properly) stick to assessing the hard skills and avoiding anything where the marking can be challenged.

It is relatively straightforward to write a marking schema that counts the words, looks for a beginning, middle and end, the use of specific techniques in the piece and good spelling, grammar, and punctuation.

It is almost impossible to get consistency if you ask people to mark on the basis of how good they though the story was.

You only need to go look at Amazon reviews of your favourite books and see the one star reviews of things you believe are masterpieces.

Just to illustrate that point. Here are a couple of one star reviews that I have taken from Amazon UK for Charles Dickens' Bleak House:

- *"I didn't finish reading it. Too much backwards & forwards, I found a job to follow the theme. I didn't enjoy it at all."*

- *"I couldn't read past the first page. It immediately gives the tedious impression of book vastly in need of editing. There is scarcely anything that is written on the first page that could not be expressed more concisely, and this to me was a bad sign: that the rest of the book would be even more verbose. So I jumped ship. I have a feeling that Dickens is really a writer that appeals to a very narrow sector of the reading public, but that we've all been hood-winked into believing him to be accessible."*

I should point out that Dickens was paid by the word and his stories were originally written as serials for weekly publications (the nineteenth century equivalent of the newpaper/magazine). This meant that he was writing to a deadline and a word count. I don't think the parts were significantly edited when they were collected into novels. That said, there are excellent characters and humbling stories. Bleak House is a lesson on litigation and not letting greed blind you to its cost.

Poetry Station
16 February 2014

I am busy crafting poetry for the third assignment of my Open University course A215 Creative Writing. Or rather I am indulging in a little displacement activity right now. However I will be back to work in a few moments.

My table set up for writing poetry, with video camera & laptop.

You will see from the picture of the table I'm using as my desk a number of things. Most useful being Stephen Fry's *The Ode Less Travelled* which is a very good introduction to poetry that I heartily recommend.

There is a video camera so that I can record myself reading the poetry out loud to listen back and refine it. This is my own take on poetry being about the sound of the thing, much more so than prose.

I think that's what makes poetry harder for many people (myself included) because it takes much more effort to craft 40 lines of poetry than it does to make thousands of words of prose.

Of course, the other main thing there is my ancient computer, which with Libre Office is giving me the canvas to paint the words on. Each draft is track changed from the previous one and saved religiously so that I can go back and restore the bits I change or cut out completely in the process.

Also there's a couple of memory sticks so that I don't lose anything I'm doing. As I type this there is yet another backup going on just to be safe.

Lastly, there is the cup of coffee to keep me effervescent...

How I write poetry
20 February 2014

Before I started studying Creative Writing course I had never tried to write poetry, even though I've written several short stories and novellas. For TMA3 of A215 I have to write 40 lines of poetry.

How I write poetry
With one exception, which was my first attempt, all of my poems have started as a freewrite on the subject, title or prompt.

Normally I discard the first paragraph of the freewrite because it is overly literal. I use words and phrases from the remainder to form the basis of the first draft of a poem.

Unlike my prose, where I typically draft in scrivener, the poetry starts on paper or a basic text editor. Subsequent drafts use the track changes feature in a word processor. This allows me to see how each poem develops.

Each draft is its own file, this starts with the 'final' text of the previous draft with changes tracked on top.

Poetry is a Spoken Form
From the second draft onward I record myself reading it on a video camera. This lets me watch it back a couple of times to hear the flow, and to check whether or not the enjambment and the general rhythm and sound works.

Sometimes the first time round I've found that I can't breathe where the line ends, so it needs played with a bit. In most cases I make amendments iteratively, within the current draft, until I am content with the sound of the poem.

Here's an example from one of the poems I didn't submit for the assignment (but still works as a poem, it was just a little short of the required line count when paired up with either of the two that I did submit).

Poetry is a Process

When teaching me how to write poetry the Open University impressed on me that poetry is a process, and it needs time to work properly.

My tutor was a published poet and she demonstrated this in the tutorials using some of her own work as examples of changes between drafts.

After the first draft I've left all my poems for at least a week and worked on other things instead. This gives it time to settle and for me to be able to look at it with fresh eyes. For subsequent drafts I leave a gap of at least a day between drafts.

Only once I am mostly fine with the flow do I share the poem with other people, so far just my wife and my fellow students. Any feedback I get then goes into the next draft which also goes through the video process.

Poetry – Bloom by James Kemp

24 February 2014

Bloom

"Splash!"

A roar over my head closes
from behind and drowns the radio.
Binoculars brought to bear, I observe
the seed embedding. It grows
a small orange blossom. Morphing
into a larger, darker flower
climbing from the point of impact.

Rain patters over the iron roof
as sods and stones strike sonorously.

The flower is gone, dissipated
in a cloud of dust, and silence
returns.

Notes

Bloom was the first full poem that I wrote, and this is the
fourth draft. It was prompted from my memory of
watching artillery shells burst when training as an
artillery forward observer (FOO) at Warcop training area
in Cumbria in 1991.

On the FOO course I gave an incorrect map
reference and the first ranging shell burst about 150m in
front of me (the wartime safety distance is 250m, in
peacetime double that).

Normally you don't see the orange flame of a bursting shell, I only saw it for an instant, and that most likely because of how close I was to the impact point.

By chance the shell landed right in the centre of the field of vision of my binoculars. Needless to say this event was accompanied by copious swearing as I ducked back down inside the trench. That was followed by "Add one thousand, repeat."

As part of my drafting process I read out the poem on video camera, so you can watch/listen to Bloom on youtube as well as read it.

https://youtu.be/1hsOw80cs-U

9 - Third Assignment

A215 – TMA3 Poetry – Chaos Monkeys
10 April 2014

This is one of two poems submitted as part of the poetry assignment for A215 Creative Writing.

Chaos Monkeys
No typewriters for these monkeys, pressing random
buttons on keyboards and boxen. There
goes the power, the server's down.

Chaos monkeys cannot read, instead they watch
Netflix, that set them free in the darkness
of the internet. Where did they lurk before?

Did they hide in the telephone
exchanges, or with gremlins somewhere
mechanical and unloved? Down dusty corridors behind
doors marked 'no entry to unauthorised personnel'.

All they want is somewhere warm, with food. Perhaps
they are refugees from a lab where they spent time
     solving puzzles
for treats, until they finally opened the door. At night they
wandered corridors, climbed ladders looking for more.

Like Pavlov's dog, they explore for food. Pressed
into service they explore the world wide web
pulling plugs on servers. Every outage earns
a reward, they google for greed.

Notes
The video on demand company, Netflix, created a
program referred to as a 'chaos monkey' to test the
resilience of their cloud computing service by randomly
switching off servers to see whether or not the service
kept working.]

You can see the original linespacing on the web
version (using a landscape monitor)

http://www.themself.org/2014/04/a215-tma3-poetry-chaos-monkeys/

Night Shift

Head shakes, eyes blink. Focus!
How did I get here?
Up all night. Hard work, physically
hard. Moving stuff, carrying, fetching,
looking after people.

Dawn came and went
home, still no sleep. On autopilot
driving through a green
tunnel, mud walls. Country
lanes. Trees covering the sunken road.

Home. How did I get here?
Zombie shuffle, surface smile. Inside
I seek sleep. Children
jumping, shouting, pleased
to see me return.

Standing outside school. How did I get here?
Don't remember leaving
the house. Children
delivered to the care of others.

Back home already? How did I get here?
Sugary, sweet tea. Steaming beside
the bed. Alarm!

Awake. Cup empty. Clock.
Four hours gone. Where did it go?

[24 lines]

Commentary

I had never written poetry, and felt uncomfortable about this section. I didn't know how to start a poem.

Nevertheless I worked through the poetry section and one of the exercises produced my first poem (Bloom - see above). On the second reading, after the tutorial and reading *The Ode Less Travelled* (Stephen Fry, 2005) it started to make sense.

The tutorial really helped me. The advice on rhyme and form made sense, I then understood that form should fit art and not the opposite (Tutor, 2014).

I did exercises with rhyming and iambic pentameter but this didn't inspire me, more work than pleasure. The 'How to' poetry from the online tutorial was really fun (Meta Poetry - see above).

I chose free verse for each of the poems submitted because it suited the subject matter and allowed me more room to use techniques like enjambment and gave more freedom on word choice than conforming to, e.g. a sonnet with ABAB rhyming and iambic pentameter (Anderson, 2006).

For inspiration I used my notebook to review ideas and freewrite. I drafted several poems but narrowed the TMA to three possibles, totalling 59 lines, which were posted to the TGF. I gave and received feedback.

Poetry Process

Most of my poems started as a freewrite, most of which was discarded. Chosen words and phrases formed the basis of the first draft. Unlike my prose, the poetry tended to start on paper.

Subsequent drafts happened on a word processor using track changes to allow me to see how each poem developed, saving each draft as a separate From the second draft onward I recorded myself reading.

Chaos Monkeys

This was the last poem I started, developed from a blog post inspired by a workshop on cloud computing architecture.

The first draft was on the train home from work. I took the idea more literally, and thought about real monkeys in data centres.

I consciously used enjambment to get double meanings from as many of the sentences as possible and tried to evoke imagery of shadows and forgotten corners, this being about behind the scenes web services and things we aren't usually conscious of.

Night Shift

This started from the TMA prompt and was called tiredness until the third draft because it draws on my wife's experience as the night sister at a local hospital.

She often comments that she doesn't remember driving home after a night shift. I hope that the short sentences and enjambment show how difficult thinking becomes when you get very tired. In particular I chose imagery that seemed blurred at first, but sharpens when it gets the focus of attention.

10 - More on poetry

Poetry Pointers
5 July 2014

Having struggled to start with when learning how to write poetry I distilled what I learnt into some pointers on writing poetry that works for me.

This is especially intended to help anyone struggling with their inner editor over whether or not their work is good enough.

Guidelines for the wise
- Poetry is a process, just like prose poems don't spring onto the page fully formed
    - ➢ expect to polish poetry through several drafts to get it just right
    - ➢ first drafts are always unpublishable, don't be discouraged by this, it gives you material that you can craft
- Poetry works best when read aloud
    - ➢ From the second or third draft record yourself reading aloud and listen back
    - ➢ where you consistently stumble change words or line breaks
    - ➢ your poetry should have a rhythm (don't confuse rhythm with rhyme)

> ➢ remember to pause at both line breaks and punctuation, it can often change the meaning, or make things delightfully ambiguous for a moment

- Rhyming isn't necessary, nor is a traditional structure or form

  > ➢ make your poetry fit the sense you want to convey, don't force a form

- the poet chooses the words, not the rhyme scheme or the form

  > ➢ use normal language and word order, write poetry for you

  > ➢ rhyme is fine if you can do it, but it is hard and can easily go wrong

- Delight the reader with misdirection, changes in meaning and clever use of words
  > ➢ make sure you still make sense

The Inner Editor

Hopefully this will help any of you considering writing poetry but having the inner editor getting in the way of submitting anything for publication.

The inner editor tells us all that our stuff isn't good enough, but usually the editor is lying to us. If you tick most of the boxes above (especially polishing multiple drafts and reading aloud) then send it in despite it all. Better for other people to read it and give you feedback than have it lurk in the back of a drawer.

Part 4 - Life Writing

11 - Learning about life writing

A215 – Life Writing – An Early Memory
24 March 2014

Life writing is a pretty wide field I've realised. I've temporarily paused trying to write TMA4 and prep for the EMA to participate in A215's 4th online tutorial.

The task here is to write three short snapshots of memories and then try to link them together with a through-line. We've not to post the original pieces to the tutorial, but rather a consolidated draft. So I thought that this would give me three ready made blog articles, but on reflection I only want to post two. Here's the first.

An Early Memory
Note: I can't precisely date this, most probably it is 1976 or 1977, because I generally recall things well from when my brother was born in Feb 1979, however the winter of discontent was 1978-9 and was marked with many power cuts. I'm sure if I asked my mum she'd give me a better guess.

It's sometime in the late 1970s, I'm about six or seven. Sitting on the multi-coloured living room carpet, it has a pattern of squares with swirly bits on the inside of them. Each of the squares has a border wide enough for a hot wheels car to use as a lane. I've got a pile of lego on the carpet and I'm sitting near the window and the door to the verandah, the area near me is vivid but the rest of the room is lost in the darkness.

Candles supplement the weak Scottish daylight which is obscured by clouds. Next to me washing hangs up drying, which is unusual as there is a drying room downstairs. My younger brother is asleep on the sofa and my Mum is helping me to build a house. I can see the thick green base tile and the red and white lego bricks forming into a house. In the dim Scottish winter night I can't play for long before it is too dark to see.

A215 – Life Writing – Initiative at Night
26 March 2014

Here's the second of the pieces I wrote for the online tutorial on life writing.

Saturday 14th December 1991

It's 3am on the second Saturday before Christmas 1991, I've been awake for 21 hours. After a day of university lectures I went with the UOTC to Redford Barracks in Edinburgh for a training camp.

Since 18:30 I have been on the Pentland Hills doing orienteering and solving problems with a team of third year cadets. We've not been good at following the approved DS solutions.

To change the tire on a land rover without a jack we ignored the planks and milk crates and instead rolled the vehicle onto its side before righting it after we'd changed the tire. Our time was the fastest, but the officer wasn't pleased.

To take a casualty across a minefield (laid with dummy mines that emit smoke if you tread on them) we simply picked up the stretcher and ran across the minefield to the designated helicopter landing site. We got a lecture about that. (Notably, some Paras did the exact same thing in Helmand almost twenty years later, and that was with real mines and a real casualty.)

About 23:00 it starts to snow, and when we cross the Pentland Hills as a gaggle with a bunch of other teams it is several inches deep and we have a snowball fight across the line of march.

My team are all pretty fit and taking this in our stride, we range up and down the column, encouraging some of the newer recruits who are obviously struggling with this unexpected night exercise.

We start some singing to raise morale, and a few minutes after we do we bump into the Colonel, who joins us for ten minutes as we march over the summit. Some snowballs follow the other column with whom we are exchanging places. The Colonel finds this amusing, but carefully avoids joining in.

Over the other side we need to spot some vehicles using night vision equipment and then re-assemble some weapons. This is followed by an indoor stint where we are asked a whole bunch of military knowledge questions. I ruin the graph showing that scores decline with sleep deprivation by scoring 100%, although the rest of the teams manage to keep to the theory.

After this, we go next door to a room with a pile of cables, headsets, batteries and some unfamiliar radio equipment. Jimmy, the Royal Signals sergeant major running the stand, briefs us that we need to assemble an automatic re-broadcast station using the pieces given.

The rest of the team turn and look at me expectantly. The bounce is wearing off, but I am still very much awake.

'Joe, you know about radios, what do we do?' asks Ian, who's in the engineer troop. I look around and a couple of the others have flopped down.

'Why don't you guys get a brew on and I'll have a look at it' I say, unstrapping the webbing that I've been carrying all evening. 'There's a flask of hot water on the top, and a burner in that pouch' I hand it over to Ian. 'Chocolate in the ammo pouches, share it round.'

Over the last two and a half years I've become an expert at looking after myself, and others, when out and about. I never go anywhere without a brew kit, chocolate to share and food for 24 hours. Weighs me down, but well worth it for unexpected jaunts like tonight.

I take control of the assorted bits of signals equipment. I've never seen this particular type of radio before, but the principles are the same as the ones I have used. Looking round the main transmitter box I find several labelled ports for leads to be attached, including a coax style connector for sending signals in and out.

By the time I'm done attaching wires and plugging in cables and headsets Ian has made a brew, passed it round with the chocolate, and boiled water to refill the flask. It's been about ten minutes and I tell Jimmy that it's done. I drink the remnants of the very strong sweet coffee Ian made and chew on a mars bar.

Jimmy gives it a quick once over and then confirms that it works by sending a message between two other similar sets on different frequencies.

We set off into the dark for our next map reference, which turns out to be a group of four ton trucks to take us back to the barracks. We can sleep, but it's only two and a half hours until breakfast!

Life Writing – Working in the Dark
31 March 2014

From the two pieces I've already posted, Early Memories & Initiative at Night and another I drafted this piece as part of the life writing tutorial for A215 Creative Writing. It has summarised the original freewrites and linked them with a through-line.

Working in the Dark

> "How many civil servants does it take to change a lightbulb?"

> "None, they prefer to work in the dark!"

As a small child I play with lego by candlelight, a power cut. I sit beside the glass door to the balcony, the rest of the room is dark and impenetrable. The multicolour swirl pattern on the carpet is vivid. The thick green base tile and the red and white lego bricks forming into a house. In the dim Scottish winter night I can't play for long before it is too dark.

Almost twenty I spend a night navigating between bases on the Pentlands to solve puzzles with a group of fellow officer cadets. After a day at university we are flung unexpectedly onto the hills. A psychological trick when we expected to spend the evening drinking in the mess. In the dark we find inventive solutions, much to the chagrin of the Directing Staff. A land rover rolled to change the wheel without a jack. We run a stretcher casualty through a minefield. This carries on all night.

We are disqualified, the solutions we found in the dark aren't approved.

Almost thirty I set up the Climate Change Levy Administration. My first day is greeted by a dark, empty office, no furniture, just a carpet. My new boss thinks the task is impossible in the time. No-one in our Department has ever run an operational case-working team, so there are no ideas about how to set one up. Less than a fortnight later I have begged, borrowed and scrounged facilities for twenty-two people, and recruited twenty people, built an IT system and got the process going. We finish two weeks early.

By forty I understand that I am at my best when working in the dark, improvising and adapting to overcome issues.

12 - Fourth assignment

Refusal

7th August 2012, Gatwick South Arrivals

I observe the next passenger. Twenty-something female, sneakers, flowing trousers, long-sleeved top showing cleavage. Slightly overweight, not fat by British standards. Probably an American.

Dirty blonde hair, rosy complexion but paler than usual for Americans. Her face has an expression of entitlement that characterises Americans in the immigration queue. They don't like to wait, nor deal with officialdom. She should be straightforward, Americans are low risk.

'NEXT!' I call.

She walks up leading with her boarding card tucked inside the passport, either she can follow instructions (a rarity) or she's a frequent traveller (more likely). Her handbag is crooked in her elbow. She tows a small 'Hello, how are you?' I ask, taking her landing card and newish US passport.

'I'm good.' She replies.

I put the landing card on the desk and feed her passport into the reader.

'So, where have you come from today?' I ask, reading the landing card.

'Toronto'. Most of the queue so far have been Canadians from the same flight.

'How long are you staying for?'

'Five and a half months.' Odd. Americans get six months without a visa, but no-one arrives with plans to do that.

'What is the purpose of your visit?' I'm still smiling at her, because I want to get her whole story before I challenge anything.

'Well, you know, I just want to see some stuff, hang out and maybe travel a bit.'

'What sort of stuff do you want to see?'

'Well I'd like to go see some movie premieres in Leicester Square, and maybe get some pictures taken with Taylor Lautner'. She names several other male actors from movies aimed at young women. Nothing I'd watch.

'So what do you do for a living?'

'I'm a webmistress.'

'And what does that involve, exactly?'

'I run a fan website for Taylor Lautner,' she says. I look at her blankly and she carries on. 'I get pictures and sighting reports and post them up for other fans to discuss in the forums.'

While she talks I flick through her passport. The US Embassy in London issued it six months ago. It only has British stamps and the other end of this trip. She continues telling me about her fantastic job.

'Would you like to see some pictures?' she asks, rummaging in her handbag.

'No, that won't be necessary.' I pause until I have her full attention again.

'Where are you staying while you're in the UK?'

'I've got a place in East London booked for a couple of months.'

'Do you have confirmation of that?'

She produces some battered A4 from her handbag. A quick glance shows the same address as the landing card. I keep the paper.

'Do you have a return ticket?'

'Uh, no. I wasn't sure exactly when I was going back. It's cheaper to buy two singles than a flexible return.'

'No problem, what funds do you have available while you are here?'

'Oh, more than enough.' She looks coy.

'How much is more than enough?' I need a number, and some proof.

'More than you can imagine.' She smiles coquettishly at me. I'm not the right man for that approach.

'I can imagine quite a lot, how much money do you have?'

She looks annoyed.

'Can I come round?' she asks, all schoolgirlish.

'OK,' I say, jumping off the chair, just in case. She comes round and holds open her handbag so that I can see the bundles of cash inside it.

'How much?' I ask.

She looks around before whispering 'Six thousand pounds'.

Definitely suspicious.

'Thanks.'

She returns to the front of the desk.

'So, is this your first trip to Britain?' I ask, knowing her UK residence permit number is written in her passport.

'No, I've been before.' Good, but she probably knows that I know.

'How long did you live here for?' I ask.

'I studied here for a couple of years.'

'What did you read and where?' I ask.

'I did a Masters with University College London in Political Philosophy.'

'When did you finish?'

'June 2011.'

That visa would have expired before her current passport was issued.

'So what have you been doing since then?'

'I did another course at London City.'

'What did you study?'

'Access to Fashion.'

'OK. Because you've had a recent visa I need to check your fingerprints.' I push the fingerprint reader forwards

Her smile fades.

'Sure.'

'Can you put your right thumb on the reader please?'

She puts her thumb on the reader and I press the button to make it go.

When it stops glowing red I say, 'Now your index finger please.'

She complies and I scan it too.

'Thank you, just a moment and the computer will match it.' I say as I am filling in a detention notice.

Melissa brightens up at the sound of the stamp, thinking that I have endorsed her passport.

'Melissa, I need to check some things before I can land you. So I need to detain you while I do that.' I hand her a slip of paper, 'This is a formal notice of detention'.

'What?' she deflates visibly, like someone has punctured her.

'I need you to take a seat while I make some enquiries.' I say, going round to where Melissa stands.

This clearly isn't going according to her plan.

'Is there anything more you need from me?' she asks.

'Not right now, just take a seat please.' I gesture towards the seating area between the two lines.

I escort Melissa to the waiting area, a fenced off collection of seats bolted to the floor in front of the immigration desks. I report to the duty Chief Immigration

Officer (CIO) in the Watch Room. That done I log in and find Melissa's student visa, which expires tomorrow. It allows her to work up to sixteen hours a week. So how has she managed to acquire £6,000 in cash?

Re-reading the paperwork I collected from her, I notice the accommodation receipt was for July and August, so she has already used half of her time. I check her passport and find an entry stamp for Canada the previous Friday, she's only been away for the weekend!

I go back to the CIO. I don't believe that she is a genuine visitor to the UK. She has a student visa and has been working more than allowed. He agrees with my assessment and proposed course of action.

I go back to the waiting area and collect Melissa.

'Bring all your belongings, we're going to collect your luggage.'

Melissa picks up her handbag from the seat.

'I've only got hand luggage,' she says.

'That's fine, we still need to go upstairs anyway.' I say. 'Follow me'.

We go past the desks to the escalators leading to baggage reclaim.

'You're sure you have no bags to collect?' I ask again.

'Yes. Just this.' She indicates her bags.

'Right, this way then.' I direct her away from the baggage reclaim through a controlled access door into a short corridor with three doors. The middle door is open.

'Through the open door please.' I say. The room is spartan, lit only by a caged fluorescent light, with bare white walls and lino floor tiles. A female immigration officer sits on one of three orange plastic chairs at the single table, all bolted to the floor.

'Melissa, we've got a few more questions for you. Please take a seat.'

'I'm not sure why I am here, I'm just an ordinary American.' Melissa replies.

'The reason you're here is that I'm not satisfied you're a genuine visitor to the UK'.

'I'm really here, and visiting, or at least I hope I am.'

'That's not what we mean. When does your student visa expire?'

'I finished the course at the end of June.'

'Yes, but when does the visa expire?'

'Oh, I think it expired last week.'

'It doesn't expire until tomorrow. Do you still have your biometric residence permit?'

'I wasn't trying to come back in as a student, I wanted to be a visitor.'

'Maybe, but you can't be a visitor while you still have a valid student visa.'

'Oh.'

'Also, I wanted to talk about the large quantity of cash in your handbag. Would you mind counting it in front of us on the table, and explaining where it came from please?'

'Do I have to?'

'Yes.'

Melissa opens her handbag. Seven inch-thiick bundles, mainly of twenty-pound notes bound by red elastic bands are stacked in the middle of the table.

'So where did you get this much cash?'

'I earned it.'

'Doing what?'

'You know, boys.'

That is all I need to confirm my suspicions.

'Melissa Duffield, I have reason to believe that you having been working in breach of your visa conditions and that you are not a genuine visitor to the UK. I am therefore refusing you leave to enter. There is no right to appeal this decision, but you may apply for a visa at a British Embassy overseas.'

Commentary

Life writing is something I read a lot of. I have a bookcase full of first-hand accounts of twentieth century warfare and social history. Some of these are straight autobiography, some have been ghost-written and others are drawn from interviews by historians.

As with previous TMAs I started several pieces in different styles to explore the range of techniques and ensure that I would be able to produce an appropriate passage. I freewrote on each TMA prompt and I also thought back on memorable incidents that I could write about.

Several threads emerged, although I rejected 'war stories' as I'd used one of those for my first TMA. I developed two promising threads, one on family history developed from the freewrite prompt 'looking at my father' and also another around having worked as a contingency immigration officer during the Olympic period in 2012.

For the family history thread I did some research. I reviewed the known family history that my father had left me when he died, I spoke to my mother about it and also looked at the discoveries I'd made since then.

The most interesting facet seemed to be my Great Great Grandfather who had been reputed to have run off with a Laird's daughter when he'd come to the village I grew up in. The facts on this revealed that he'd committed adultery and fraud (Kemp,2011).

For the other thread I re-read my journal which had accompanied me to Gatwick (Kemp,2012). Each shift I worked at the airport I recorded details of any interesting people that I'd met over the course of the day. I picked two of these and amalgamated them to try and ensure that personal confidentiality was retained.

This gave me the opportunity to use some fictional techniques, especially around creating characters from life (Anderson,2006). I made sure that the procedural parts didn't contain any classified material, I found that the Home Office have published some of the immigration procedures (Great Britain,2013).

Both threads had a first draft of the required length prepared when I'd finished reading the chapters in the course book. In re-reading these I realised that there was more research required on the family history front to fill in some of the gaps, even with that I would still need to extrapolate and fictionalise a lot to make a compelling narrative from it.

While I felt that this could be acceptable as a piece of life writing I believed that it would be better to progress with the other piece. The immigration story also needed fictional elements, but these were a result of combining two separate incidents (an American student over-stayer and another young woman working as an escort while on a student visa).

I posted the third draft of Refusal to the TGF, and after feedback from other students I revised the draft taking into account their comments. I then read it out loud and posted the revised fifth draft again. As well as receiving feedback I also commented on the work of other students.

13 - more life writing

Cub Camp 2014
21 July 2014

I got back yesterday evening from a two night camp with Clark Pack of 5th Reigate (Merstham) cub scouts. We were up at Jordan Heights, a little piece of unspoilt wilderness hidden on the back of Reigate Hill about 100m from the A217.

The campsite is appropriately spartan. The facilities are geared for adventure rather than comfort. This is a good thing when you are scouting. There are some custom built outdoor cooking facilities, a hut for storage and as a backstop against inclement weather.

There are also air rifle and archery facilities with a trained instructor available. The campsite is a couple of flattened areas both bigger than our scout hall and it is set in the woods on the side of Reigate Hill.

There are other facilities too, and you can see the details on the Jordan Heights scout campsite website.

We got there on Friday afternoon and hauled all our kit up the steps to the camping area. The cubs shared three tents and the leaders had three also.

Although us leaders had a little more space each than the boys did.

One of the parents asked about what our plans were for bad weather. Akela's answer? "We've got a programme and we'll stick to it." We did.

Dinner was pizza in the pizza oven. A metal bin bricked into a fire pit with racking inside. We had pizza bases and the cubs made up their own pizzas from a selection of toppings. Mostly these went well, but we had to refuel the fire during the process and four of the pizzas ended up crispier and darker than desired.

After dinner we got the cubs into the hut as it had started to rain, but not before Akela took them on a tour of the campsite and they managed to lose a football into the bushes...

There was a plan for this part of the camp. We all, leaders included, decorated some plain white scarves far camp. We also learnt how to do the friendship knot that Bear Grylls usually uses on his scarf. There were some fantastic designs done. We also had some cake and gave one of the cubs a birthday present as it was his birthday.

As expected it took a little while to get all the cubs settled down in their tents and off to sleep. This wasn't helped by the heat. However we got them all asleep eventually.

Friday night was the second consecutive night of thunderstorms. All the tents waterproofing were thoroughly tested, the newest one not standing up very well. It was fine overnight, but one of the cubs stood up in the morning and got soaked. While I helped cook breakfast on the fire the new tent was taken down and replaced with our spare.

7/7 London Bombings Remembered
7 July 2015

Ten years ago the last successful terrorist spectacular was about to happen in London. 52 people were murdered by suicide bombers in one of the worst terrorist attacks in mainland Britain.

Thankfully the repeat attempt a fortnight later didn't work, nor did the attempted car bombing at Glasgow airport. All the other attempts in the UK have been much lower key and, barring the murder of Drummer Rigby, not successful. That said British people have been killed overseas, last week's tragedy in Tunisia being a terrible example of the willingness of extremists to go for soft targets.

The 7/7 attacks are probably the only terrorism that I've seen from where it happened when it was going on. My job at the time was head of fire control policy. So I was responsible for government policy on how the Fire & Rescue Service dealt with major incidents.

Largely that was around coordination and interoperability rather than incident command, the Chief Fire Officers dealt with the last. On checking, my work notebook doesn't have an entry for 7th July 2005 (in fact it has a three week gap finishing one notebook on the 6th and starting the next on 27th July 2005)

When the first bomb went off I was already at my desk in central London. The initial report (which I got within minutes of the explosion) was of a power surge in the London Underground. Initially, we had no thought of terrorism. However the Fire Emergency Incident Centre was stood up. One of my team went to help out.

As more information became available the picture became clearer that we were dealing with multiple bombs. Early on I called the Fire Minister's private secretary to tell him what I knew. Although things escalated and John Prescott went to COBR and was directly supported by the FEIC. At one point we had eight major incidents running simultaneously, mainly because each end of a tube tunnel was being handled as a major incident.

I largely watched and waited. Observing for lessons and also calling the national command centre to get them stood up. I also maintained the link with the Fire Minister's private office (Jim Fitzpatrick MP was the Minister, he was a former firefighter and FBU NEC member).

At one point I was asked to find out how well London Fire Brigade were coping with things, and my answer was that they were doing very well. I didn't actually check with LFB because I reckoned that they had enough on their plate, but I knew that the FEIC was talking to them and my contacts there weren't reporting problems.

Mainly I spent my time accounting for the project team and also keeping in touch with my wife who was six months pregnant and busy getting people out of hospital beds in Hillingdon Hospital so that there was space to admit the injured.

It took a few hours to account for the 90 people in the project team. Most of them had been en route and so we're mired in the chaos. All the Fire service secondees were put to work in the FEIC. The consultants were sent away and the civil servants helped where they could. By late lunchtime everyone not directly helping with coordination was sent home.

I finally went home at about 1730 and it was the emptiest I've ever seen Victoria station. The few commuters were outnumbered by armed police, PCSOs and station staff and there were loads of trains. In fact in their effort to ease people home there were about three times as many trains as normal stopping at my home station. I didn't need to wait at all and there were empty seats as we left the station.

There was a sort of post apocalyptic feel, desertion rather than chaos, about the Victoria area of central London. You don't get that even in the wee small hours, there's always traffic and people hanging about. But on the evening of 7th July 2005 no one was hanging about, even the armed police looked alert and purposeful in their patrolling.

The next day I did speak to the Assistant Commissioner of LFB about it. Oddly they'd had a very quiet day, much less busy than usual (incident response aside). The initial explosions were all underground so they'd only had six 999 calls about them.

By the time people that had seen it reached the surface there were LFB crews on the scene. After that they found there were very few 999 calls, people seemed to have been more careful and also thought twice before calling for help.

Presumably they could see that responding to the bombings and rescuing people was higher priority than their minor issues. Very unusually there were no prank calls or false alarms.

With luck, nothing like this will ever happen again in the UK. Although one cannot ever be complacent about that.

Car crash

30 September 2015 -

Yesterday morning I had a bit of an altercation with a volvo. Having just dropped Alexander off at his school, I was taking Lucy to her swimming lesson in Oxted. The weather was clear, bright sun and dry when the car crash happened.

Car Crash

As I went down Pendell Road towards Hawthorns school the black volvo pulled out of the school entrance in front of me. I just had time to start braking before impact. Fortunately I'd not being going that fast because I'd just come round a bend. It was probably slower than 20 mph car crash into the side of the volvo.

Both my front airbags went off, and my glasses disappeared. The air was full of an acrid used fireworks smell. I could see some residual dust settling in the morning sunlight. The whole front of the car looked crumpled, but not as far as my footwell.

I had a moment of disbelief before I reacted. When I did I turned round to check on my daughter. Lucy was strapped in the back. As I turned she started crying, or maybe I just became aware of it then. I tried to reassure her, but couldn't reach to unstrap her.

I undid my own seat belt and tried to open the door. It wouldn't move, the car crash must have bent the frame. So I kicked it and it opened.

That was when I realised that the engine was still running. So I switched it off and put the keys in my pocket. I still couldn't see my glasses, but gave up looking for them to get Lucy.

I ran round the back of my car and got Lucy out. She was distressed but seemed OK. She got herself out of the seat when I unclipped her harness. I picked her up and cuddled her. She stopped crying almost immediately. Then she looked at our car and said "our car is damaged"!

It dawned on me standing between the two cars that I hadn't seen any movement from the other car. So I opened the rear door and shouted to ask if they were OK. No answer.

Still carrying Lucy I went round to the passenger side of the other car and pulled open the door. A woman was sitting very still in the driving seat. My first thought was that she was badly hurt, or even dead. However she responded to my 'are you all right?'

She was clearly shocked by the car crash, and me appearing with a little girl in my arms probably didn't make her feel any better. I gave her some space to get out.

A man offered to help move the cars out of the way. He'd been coming the other way from me and got out of his car when he saw the car crash. I suggested that he take some pictures first just in case we needed them for the police or insurance. I gave him my camera and went back to my car to look for my glasses.

By this time a few other people were milling about offering to help. There was also a queue of traffic backing up. Someone found my glasses for me and the chap who took the pictures moved my car. A Fire & Rescue Service officer turned up randomly and helped to direct the clearing of the road.

Over on the other side of the road I kept out of the way with the other driver. She was mortified by having caused the crash. We exchanged contact details and reassured each other that we'd survived it. Not such a big deal.

Another mum from the school also pulled up and offered to take us somewhere. The Bursar also came out in his high vis jacket to see if he could help. They helped look after Lucy for a few moments while I recovered some things I knew we'd need soon from the car.

I didn't catch the lady's name, but she was really helpful and friendly and took us both home.

Fantastic Service from Insurance Companies

I have to say that both insurance companies involved were really helpful. I was on the phone for over an hour. But the end result was that I had a resolution for the claim, my car was a total loss and they offered me money for it. I also got sorted out with a rental car until I got the money I needed for a replacement.

My insurance was with Allianz through the AA as a broker. The other driver was insured by Admiral. Admiral called me directly and apologised for the car crash, accepted liability and were going to offer me a settlement.

If I hadn't already called my own insurer then it might have saved me some time. I'm impressed by them both.

Part 5 - Bringing it together

14 - Learning about publication

A215 – Creative Writing Assignments so far
9 April 2014

TMA4 for A215 Creative Writing is back. All that remains is TMA5 and the end of module assessment (EMA). Both of these are a free choice from the three taught types of writing, short fiction, poetry and life writing.

Before I started the course I had mostly written fiction, in the novelette to novel range for length, none of which you'd reasonably describe as short in OU terms (somewhere in the 2,000 word range).

My first assignment for A215 ended up as life writing, I found it easier to write short bits about memories than to condense fiction down to the correct word count (and I'm very good at editing things down).

The second assignment was short fiction, and I managed to write a half-decent story for it. *Rounds* is the beginning of a longer story that I still might write, lots of background got generated and ideas for continuation. When I'm done with the course and have edited my novel into something presentable then I may well come back to it.

Rounds wasn't the only story though, it was at least the fourth that I planned and started to draft. Of the others two were way too long and complicated to get something reasonable out in 2,000 words; at least at my current skill level for fiction. Another was too short and lacked some dramatic tension (possibly because of the situation rather than its length).

Poetry came next, and it scared me. The Big Red Book didn't really help much with that, I found it was laid out wrong, either that or it was assuming a whole background in English Literature that I didn't have.

If you'd already deconstructed poetry at university level I dare say that you'd have been okay with the way the book introduced writing it. However I've been doing a Business & Leadership degree, so I haven't been taking poems apart.

However two things saved me, one of which was the fact that my tutor is a poet and she ran an excellent tutorial that demystified it. Stephen Fry's book 'An Ode Less Travelled' was also a much better introductory work, it didn't assume any prior knowledge, was written in a conversational style (I could hear Stephen being both patient and witty) and also explained the technical bits very clearly.

Life writing was the fourth assignment, and I started a couple of things. I intended to do some biographical bits based on some of the family history research that I've done over the last few years.

I thought a piece related to the Family Mystery posts (Family Mystery pt.2) I'd done would be interesting to read and also provide me with a good opportunity to show that I'd used the techniques from the Big Red Book. That was fine, but I lost my planned study day because my daughter vomited on the childminder ten minutes after I dropped her off.

After that my work got unexpectedly busy and someone outside my chain promised top management that we'd launch a beta version of the software we're working on at the time when I expected a second alpha to be ready for checking and accreditation.

So I fell back on something much easier to write and rapidly knocked it through a couple of drafts. This got me something comfortably acceptable for the deadline.

Now though I'm faced with a dilemma. Looking at my marks the thing that scored best was the poetry, it isn't hugely better marks wise, but it scraped into the next category of pass from the other stuff (which was all at the upper end).

The range of marks is 8 percentiles, with the two life writing TMAs being at the bottom of the range, the fiction a couple of percentiles above them, and four below the poetry.

Once I'd done the poetry I realised that it was easier than I thought, but I still didn't expect to be doing any more of it. Now I'm sitting here thinking that I may well write several more poems for TMA5 and perhaps the EMA (although I'm less certain of that, I have more words to play with there and could well edit down one of the spare stories from TMA2, incorporating the lessons from the BRB and the feedback from earlier assignments).

15 - Fifth assignment

Geek Poetry – New Poetry Genre?
28 April 2014

So for TMA5 of A215 I've chosen the poetry option and written a three poem sequence provisionally titled 'Castles in the Cloud' which is some very geeky poetry about cyber security.

This is works for me, even if the other folk on the course are pretty much English Lit folk who aren't geeks. That makes getting feedback hard, but not impossible.

What I am struggling with is the other part of the assignment which is to research suitable publications that I could potentially submit the poetry too.

There is a fair list of general poetry magazines at http://www.poetrylibrary.org.uk which is good enough for the purpose of the assignment. However I wanted to find the sort of place that would appreciate both the language and the underlying geekery of the work.

My Google fu has deserted me on this, either that or I've created a whole new genre of poetry (which I'm somewhat sceptical about).

So here's an appeal. Do you know of any other poetry out there about the mechanics of the Internet or computing in general? Are there other polymath poets that fuse science and art?

Castles in the Cloud

Laying Siege

Unsuspecting users are unaware of spam
silently suborning their systems. Malware lurks,
waiting for the one in a million. Click
conscripted computers, zombies
in the 'bot-net horde, pillaging
user credentials and sending more spam.

Each zombie sends tens of millions
of emails before they too are cleansed.
One day the hordes will swell,
the tide sweeping away all defences.
Then the zombie apocalypse will infect us all.

[11 lines]

Castles in the Sky

Fortresses nestle in their own cloud, keeping out trojans.
    Patterned
on mediaeval concentric rings. Each level increasingly
    secure.
Guarded by daemons, the inner keep treasures personal
data. Identities, keys to unlock unseen riches from
    numbers
normally encased in dull plastic. The cloud's silver lining.

Thickness is not measured in feet of stone, but bits
of encryption. It weathers badly, today's granite is next
decade's sand. Foundations built on a chain
of trust rather than bedrock. These walls can scale,
Hydra-like new servers spawn when the load becomes
    too heavy.

Attacking the cloud is Herculean to Quixotic,
the rewards are certainly legendary.

        [12 lines]

Firewall

I'm a simple packet sniffing firewall
building trust by transparent inspection,
plain http or nothing at all.

A serious purpose not to be hindered,
security is an important mission
for a simple packet sniffing firewall.

Absolutely every packet must be read,
without encryption or obfuscation.
Plain http or nothing at all.

Odd or unreadable packets are dropped,
it takes only the slightest suspicion.
I'm a simple packet sniffing firewall.

No complex protocol can be tunnelled,
neither SSL nor db connection.
Plain http or nothing at all.

I listen on port 80 carefully prepared
to deal malware's ultimate rejection.
I'm a simple packet sniffing firewall,
plain http or nothing at all.

[19 lines]

Notes

This poem was inspired by a bridge between security zones on a cloud hosting platform that rejects the usual secure connections and forces everything to pass through in plain http (i.e. unencrypted plain text only) so that it can tell whether or not there is any unauthorised traffic trying to pass in or out of the secure hosting zone.

Commentary

The thrust of TMA5 is around writing for publication, and editing your work so that it meets publication guidelines for the publications that you intend to submit it to.

Part 2 - Report

Initial Search

I looked for a suitable publication before choosing whether to write prose or poetry. My search criteria were for a publication with:

1.   submission guidelines online; and
2.   a traditional print version.

I felt that the course material had more traditional routes in mind (Anderson,2006). I also rationalised that print publications submission guidelines would be stricter because production costs are significant.

General Findings

I found dozens of publication websites using a links in the TMA guidance notes, a search engine and publications that I already knew. Many publications submission guidelines were vague on content, requiring reading the publication. This seemed like a good marketing ploy! Common features of submission guidelines were:

- Length (usually an upper limit);
- Unpublished material (some took reprints);
- Whether or not simultaneous submissions to other publications were allowed;
- Number of pieces submitted in parallel;
- Less common were warnings against certain material, typically erotica and/or genre fiction.

Almost every publication took electronic submissions and did not specify layout or formatting (although several specified file formats). Only one took submissions exclusively on paper (Rialto, 2014).

Selection of Granta
My initial search, combined with handling a copy at the March Day School, led me to select Granta. As a magazine of new writing it publishes a variety of art forms (Granta,2014). I acquired three copies of Granta and read them as further background.

Each of the issues I read had a specific theme. The works in the issue had a clear link to that theme, although the themes chosen were broad enough so that covered a range of material. For example, issue 82 was titled 'Life's Like That' and contained a collection of life writing, poetry and pictures related to the surprises that life brings.

Choice of Form
After I'd had TMA4 marked I finally decided that I was going to submit a sequence of poetry. In part this was

because I wanted to experiment further with the form and use a closed form with a rhyming scheme as well as free verse.

I started with a villanelle on a cyber-security related theme (prompted by my job, designing secure digital services for government).

The constraints imposed by the form made it trickier than the free verse at first, I found myself counting syllables rather than just listening to the flow. I was also conscious not to force the rhyme or allow the form to dictate word choice.

The sequence was written and posted to the TGF and feedback was both given and received. The whole sequence was drafted using the same process that I used for poetry for TMA3. The only difference was that for 'Firewall' I used a spreadsheet to count syllables by putting each syllable in its own cell and counting the non-blanks for each line. I also used a column to track the rhyme schema. This was fiddly but it worked well.

Modifications to Suit Granta
I did not modify after drafting the sequence as I had chosen the publication before I produced the work. However I did choose to write a sequence because Granta produced themed issues. Granta is currently closed to submissions, otherwise I would shorten the sequence to meet the maximum 40 lines, by removing the closing couplet on 'Castles in the Cloud'.

16 - End of Module Assessment

Introduction – Hunting Nazis

26 May 2014

I've written a short story for the End of Module Assessment (EMA) for A215 Creative Writing. The target word count was 2,500 with an upper limit of +10%. The first draft weighed in at 5k words, double the target length. However some of this was because although I plotted it I needed to tell myself the story in the first draft. Once I got to the end it was much easier to re-edit and take out some of it.

The central premise is that Reggie and Dot (from the earlier story Planting the Past) have been hunting down nazis guilty of war crimes against the members of the French resistance and SOE agents supporting the network that they were both part of during World War Two. The story takes place in Berlin in 1953 when they are tying up the last few loose ends.

There are a couple of supporting characters, Paul, another ex-resistance fighter, but one that Dot (called Nancy by him as that was her code name) doesn't trust, she's convinced that he betrayed people to the Germans. He was arrested and deported to Berlin by the Gestapo as they left France in September 1944. Somehow he managed to survive this and the fall of

Berlin to the Soviets and then establish a nightclub in a converted public air raid shelter near the Potsdamerplatz. One of his employees, a barman named Gustav is an ex-SS rifleman attached to the unit lead by SS Captain Hechte in the final days of the Reich. Reggie and Dot are looking to recover a relic stolen by Hechte and to confirm his death in May 1945 at the hands of the soviets.

There are also a couple of friendlies from their SOE days, still employed by British Intelligence but now spying on the soviets with the help of Paul and his nightclub. Their worry is that Reggie and Dot's activities might scare off the Soviet officers they've been blackmailing if they are too blatant.

No spoilers, so that's as much as I can say other than that it all comes to a climax in an abandoned bunker under the Soviet zone.

Hunting Nazis

Berlin, March 1953

The rain washed the rubble in the yellow glow of the headlights as Reggie stopped outside one of the few remaining buildings in central Berlin.

I got out of the car and waited for Reggie to join me. Dance music, talk and laughter leaked from the building. We're near the Potsdamerplatz where the British zone meets the Soviet zone.

'What exactly brings us here, Reggie?'

'Paul.'

'Merde!'

'That's no language for a lady!' Reggie chuckled.

'You know how I feel about him. I still don't know whose side he was on.'

'Paul's mainly, but he'll help us. I guarantee it.'

'Have you got any other surprises lined up?'

'Darling, how could you think such a thing? Am I not completely honest?'

'That doesn't stop you springing surprises.'

Paul was keener to see us than I was to see him. Steps brought us down into an anteroom with a bar, where Paul stood holding a champagne glass. On the bar a silver cooler stood full with ice. Behind the bar was a muscular tall blond in PT kit who'd not be out of place on a vaulting horse.

'Nancy! Reggie! Fancy seeing you here!' Paul said, his eyes and face lighting up in what seemed like genuine surprise.

'Paul. Well met.' Reggie said, nodding and bowing slightly.

I kept back and said nothing, but smiled when he looked at me. Playing games is how I survived three years of war and eight years of an even more dangerous peace.

'Have some champagne.' Paul motioned, and the barman immediately produced two more glasses. 'Gustav, these are old comrades of mine.'

'Jawohl, mein Herr.' Gustav said, nodding at us both.

'This is no coincidence Paul, I came to see you specially.' Reggie said, taking the glass from the bar. 'I wanted to make sure that you were well.'

'I'm better than that Reggie.'

'This is your place?'

'It is, let me give you a tour, and then we can catch up on old times.'

As we went through the doors furthest from the stairs I got in close to Reggie and took his arm.

'Gustav's ex SS, I saw his tattoo'. I hissed.

'Well don't show him yours.' Reggie said.

Paul interrupted to point out key features of his establishment. I paid close attention and let Reggie do all the talking.

We went through some doors. I wasn't ready for what hit me. We stood at the top of some stairs in a large well lit dance hall. A band played and blonde waitresses tended packed tables.

The tour ended in a private room. The walls featured prints of a rural idyll that I didn't believe had ever existed. I deliberately sat on the same sofa as Reggie, so that I was as far from Paul as possible.

Paul claimed that the Gestapo arrested him and brought him to Berlin when they left France in September 1944. He'd exploited that even the most ardent Nazis could see the war was ending.

In the aftermath Paul bought properties from their desperate former owners. Most were grateful for an opportunity to get away from the Soviets. The basements became the club. Where Paul got the money remained vague. He'd sold everybody to everyone else during the war. I'd always played dumb around him, letting Reggie do all the talking continued that.

I addressed Paul with my biggest smile, 'I'm just off to powder my nose.'

I went to the Ladies and sat at the mirror, discreetly looking around me. Within moments two women joined me. My German came back easily.

'You are new here.' the brown eyed girl said.

'Just arrived. You?' I asked her

'I've been working here two weeks.' She said.

'You work here?'

'All the women here work.'

The penny dropped. 'Does it pay well?'

'Well enough, although the Soviets are pigs.'

'You don't like them?'

'Of course not, I remember when they came and forced themselves on us.'

'I missed that.'

'You were very lucky.'

'I was somewhere just as bad.' I didn't tell her it was Belsen.

I followed the girls back, the band still played, and the two British officers I'd spotted were deep in conversation. I knew them both. The RAF Squadron Leader was the pilot that flew me to France. The army Major was a liaison officer.

'Hello gentlemen, mind if I join you?' I said sitting down anyway, grinning.

'Nancy! How the devil are you?' the Major cried.

'I'm all the better for seeing you, Henri.' I said. 'And you too, Blanket!'

'What brings you to Berlin then?' Squadron Leader Blanchard asked.

'Can't a girl go places without a reason?'

'Of course she can, but we know you Nancy.' Henri said.

'The two of you are pretty thick here too, not a coincidence is it?'

'You can't teach an old dog new tricks.' Henri said.

'Me too, and I could use a hand.' I said.

'Only cloaks here, nothing sharp or hard.' Blanchard said.

'We don't want to scare the horses.' Henri said.

'What about old Nazis? Are they fair game?' .

'Of course, no love for the Boche.' Henri said.

'But keep it away from the reservation.' Blanchard said.

'Thanks, you've been most helpful, I must get back.'

Reggie and I went outside for a walk and a talk.

'So what's next?' I said.

'You remember Hauptsturmfuhrer Hechte? He was in Berlin when it fell.'

'Do you think he's still alive?'

'No. But he brought a relic that I want to return. It's not far from here at all. Gustav is going to come out and help us.'

'But he's a Nazi. What makes you think he'll want to help us?'

'A former Nazi. He dislikes the Soviets, and the relics are in the Soviet zone. Are you ready for a quiet walk in the woods?'

'Of course.' I was always ready, I had a dagger and a Welrod silenced pistol.

Just after midnight Gustav appeared.

'You want to go into the Soviet sector?' Gustav said, in German.

'Yes, we want bunker 38, about one hundred metres from the Hitler Bunker.' Reggie said, in flawless unaccented German.

'I know it.'

'Give me your hand.' Reggie held his hand out to Gustav.

Gustav took Reggie's hand in his own. As soon as Reggie had a firm grip of Gustav's hand I saw Gustav's eyes roll up in their sockets. Gustav knelt involuntarily and gasped. Awe shone from his face. He knelt on the wet ground and stared up until Reggie stepped back and bade him to rise.

'Come on Gustav, we've got a relic to recover.'

The rubble wasn't as clear on the Soviet side of the line as it was on the British side. The Russians only cleared roads or to extract valuable things. There were piles of rubble where the buildings had been.

As we crossed one of these areas, Gustav slipped. The skittering stones sounded deafening in the dark.

'Wer da?' came a shout, accompanied by a metallic clunk as the sentry made his weapon ready.

We kept still and silent.

'Wer da?' again, followed by a pale torch glow in front of us. I started to perspire, despite the cold, as the beam passed over us. I counted seconds in my head. The torch glow moved away, paused and then came back for a second sweep.

Two minutes so far. This time it was just in front of us and when it passed to our left it switched off.

A brief snatch of German conversation, the Volkspolizei thought it was an animal.

We stood in an old doorway and listened before we attempted to enter the sewer system. We were 150 yards inside the Soviet sector.

Gustav went first, and easily hooked opened the manhole cover. I ran silently in my rubber soled boots.

The hole was black, I could just see a ladder. I dropped in, finding the lower rungs by feel. The smell surprised me, it was rust and oil.

It was ten rungs down before I got to the bottom, and I stepped left, keeping a hold on the ladder. Reggie did the same when he came down. There was a faint clang as Gustav replaced the cover before joining us.

'We go this way' Gustav said, using his torch to light the way.

We went parallel to the border until we came to a T junction. The smell was thicker in the new tunnel, rainwater washed effluent in from nearby drains. There was a wide path on one side with a railing to stop people falling into the stream. Painted on the wall were directions to previously important places. A short distance away from the junction we stopped at a side tunnel with 38 painted on the wall.

'This is it.' Gustav said.

'Let's go in.' Reggie said.

I hung back, Gustav had been involved on the wrong side of this. I pulled the Welrod from its hiding place, checked it was ready and tucked it into my waistband.

The bunker door swung open noiselessly. Gustav turned the lights on. We couldn't see straight in until we went round the blast walls. Inside were four rooms and a spiral staircase going down. The doors all lay open, and there was no sign of a hasty departure nor looting.

'Looks like you had an orderly withdrawal' I said.

'Yes. We were here until we heard that Hitler had fallen. After that we went West through the Tiergarten with others and broke out of the city.'

So were Hauptsturmfuhrer Hechte's relics left behind, or did those go too?'

An ominous clang rang through the bunker. I whirled around and stepped into the closest doorway.

'Kameraden!' shouted Gustav, both at me and whoever closed the bunker door. 'We're all friends, together against the godless Soviets.'

I kept the gun hidden, but remained wary. Who else was here and why?

'Come forward and be seen, slowly.' Reggie shouted in German, our apparent lingua franca.

A face peered round the blast wall, another blonde blue eyed specimen. The hair at his temples more white than blonde. He gingerly stepped round the blast wall, keeping his hands in front of him, palms out.

'Who are you?' asked Reggie.

'Hans Schneider, an old comrade of Gustav's.'

'Well, I'm pleased to meet you, you can call me Reggie' Reggie offered his hand to Hans with a smile.

Schneider took Reggie's proffered hand and shook it. Just an ordinary handshake.

'I understand that you knew Hauptsturmfuhrer Hechte?' Reggie asked.

'Unfortunately the Soviets killed him when they took Berlin.' Schneider said.

That matched our information, but sounded wrong. I looked again at Schneider, and the likeness hit me. How many other old comrades were out there? Or worse, in here already?

'We heard that he'd found some interesting relics that protected those blessed by them?' Reggie said. 'We were wondering if they could be of use against our common enemy. Would you know about that?'

'We could discuss it more comfortably downstairs, there's an officers' lounge.'

We all went down, Gustav and Schneider leading the way. The rooms down here had the same basic plan. The officers' lounge had bunk beds against one wall and a large chart of the war situation on 1 May 1945 on another. It appeared that only four of us were in the bunker, unless someone else was at the entrance.

'So you seek help in defeating the communists?' Schneider asked.

'I understood that Hauptsturmfuhrer Hechte found a method, but hadn't worked out how to implement it.

I've spent seven years tracking him down since I first heard the story in 1946.' Reggie said.

'Perhaps the story you heard was exaggerated. If Hauptsturmfuhrer Hechte had found something that powerful, surely Berlin wouldn't have fallen?' Schneider said.

'Mein Herr, perhaps you could show him, I can vouch for him being a true friend.' Gustav said.

'Ach, very well. Will you promise not to go public with any of this, nor to let it fall into the hands of either the Americans or the Soviets.' Schneider said.

'I promise.' Reggie said.

Schneider bid us to follow him. Gustav remained. Reggie and I followed Schneider to the room furthest from the stairs. The reinforced steel door showed signs of being well maintained and swung open easily. Against the walls were neat rows of wooden crates, each stencilled with its contents. In the centre two crates were stacked like an altar with an ornate jewelled gold and glass box on top. It seemed to glow faintly from reflected light.

'It's a reliquary from a Monastery in the Northern Caucasus, we picked it up from some Armenian Orthodox priests in the Autumn of 1942. They used it to bless their congregation in a ritual called Matagh every Easter by sacrificing a lamb.' Schneider said.

'It needs animal sacrifices to work?' Reggie said, stepping up to the reliquary.

'They blessed some panzers with a lamb each when we arrived. Those tanks survived the battles unscathed.'

'May I?' Reggie asked, gesturing his intent to pick up the reliquary.

'Of course.' Schneider said.

Reggie picked it up and turned it round in his hands, a look of concentration on his face was followed by one of disgust. 'You sacrificed people to this idol didn't you?'

'We ran out of lambs, but there were plenty of soviet prisoners.'

Reggie looked at me and nodded. I was still in the doorway, behind Schneider. I stepped in closer pulling the Welrod pistol from of my waistband.

'I suppose it was helping your war effort.' Reggie said, keeping Schneider's attention on him.

I put the muzzle practically on the back of his neck and squeezed the trigger.

The silenced shot echoed, like someone had dropped a heavy book onto the concrete floor. Schneider/Hechte went down in a spray of blood, leaving a red oval on the ceiling in front of him. As he fell I pulled back the action to put another bullet into the chamber, five shots left.

'Gustav?' I asked Reggie.

He shook his head. 'They corrupted this with human sacrifices.' He said, holding up the reliquary and shaking his head. 'Philistines.'

'Can you fix it?'

'It'll never be the same again, best to destroy it.'

'Nein' Hechte moaned from the floor, trying to push himself up towards Reggie.

'He's not dead!' Reggie said, stepping back from a questing hand.

My second bullet hit the middle of his back, where I expected his heart to be. I cocked the Welrod again. Four shots left.

Hechte fell back down, but didn't stop, he was still moving. How could this be?

Reggie hit Hechte with the reliquary, glass shattered and blood flew. Hechte grabbed Reggie's left leg. Blood ran from the reliquary, a reservoir inside must have broken, there was too much to have come just from Hechte's head.

My third round went into Hechte's head. He went down, letting go of Reggie. Reggie dropped the reliquary.

'I think the second bullet to his brain did the trick, Reggie.'

'Maybe, but I want to be sure.'

When we got out of the bunker I found Blanket and Henri to enlist their help. They knew we'd been tracking war criminals involved in murdering SOE agents. I told them that Hechte had resisted arrest and I'd had to shoot him. They organised a clean up squad to help us.

Reggie made sure that Hechte was cremated quickly, he never was one with taking chances. He put the remains of the reliquary in the furnace too, including the glass he'd swept up and the blood covered carpet.

'How could you be sure of Gustav's help?' I asked Reggie as we lay safely in a hotel bed together.

'I had a long chat with him while you were talking to your old friends.'

'You hypnotised him!'

'You saw that yourself. I knew it would work because we'd spoken. He was unhappy about things his comrades did during the war.'

'He must have volunteered for the SS though.'

'He was an impressionable 18 year old with eight years of brainwashing in the Hitler Youth. You remember what it was like here then.'

Commentary

I chose to write a short story for my EMA because my preferred form of creative writing is fiction. I chose not to present the opening chapters of my novel because I felt that a complete story crafted to the word limits was a better showcase for the techniques that I have learnt. Long form fiction is quite different from short fiction and is not a specific taught form. I've written 76,000 words towards a speculative fiction novel, which is not yet complete. I recognise through my experience with TMA2 that complete short fiction is a significant challenge.

Creating Characters

I used three of the four methods of creating characters, several were biographical e.g. Paul is based on Henri Dericourt, suspected of being a double, or even triple, agent working for SOE and the Germans (and perhaps also MI6). Gustav is based on a real SS volunteer. Some were pure invention and most were a combination drawing on real historical people and layering on invention to suit the plot.

The main characters in the story presented were inspired by a very short piece written for the first online tutorial (see Planting the Past above). Further inspiration came from a book that I read and reviewed (Rita Kramer's *Flames in the Field*) as part of my research for life writing. *Flames in the Field* tracks the fate of four SOE agents arrested by the nazis during the war. After the war another SOE agent enlisted the help of army officers to find out what happened to all the SOE agents that didn't return.

Settings
The setting came from a spy novel I read years ago which stuck in my mind, and I searched the internet to find out details of nazi bunkers and the fall of Berlin, some of this is copied on my website (http://www.full-moon.info/doku.php/dg/berlin). I have also had years of reading military history and about the details of nazi war crimes. I used this knowledge to help flesh out the plot and background.

Conflict
As mentioned previously, a vital part of a good story is the 'character + conflict = plot' equation (Anderson,2006) so when outlining stories I took care to ensure that there was conflict built in to the structure. I followed my notebook approach in this.

Point of View
I also spent some time considering the narrator as discussed in Chapters 7 (first person) & 8 (third person). I considered multiple first person viewpoints, but the word count constraint made this impractical.

Show vs Tell

I determined to show as much as possible and use tell sparingly. The story needed to use dialogue and action with emotion shown from the spoken words, or the actions of characters (Browne & King, 2004).

I used my normal approach for fiction. This is to plan the events in rough outline, write some descriptive text about the characters so that I understood who they were and why they were needed for the plot. I then mulled over the ideas in my head and wrote them in detail scene by scene until I had completed the story as plotted. The first draft, excluding the notes on character, plot and background, weighed in at just over 5,000 words. Double the stated word limit.

I had a brief spell of illness between the first and second drafts, which prevented me from working for almost two weeks. I went through the draft and tidied it up, reading dialogue and tightening it up, removing surplus description and ensuring that all the text was doing something to tell the story. At this stage the draft was down to 3,881 words, still 50% more than allowed.

A second prune a couple of days later brought the word count down still further, but it was still 700 words over the upper limit. Nevertheless I posted this to the TGF in the hope that some other students might have time to comment on it and offer feedback.

17 - More on studying

Six Steps to an Awesome Assignment
10 August 2014

> **"*Academics are like vampires...*"**

Like almost everything in life there is a knack to doing well in Open University assignments (and this probably carries through to other assignments too).

Knowing your stuff will get you a pass, but putting these tips into practice will turn that into a good pass, or even a distinction. This is my experience and things I've picked up from tutors and other students over the course of six modules from Level 1 through to Postgraduate.

OU tutors are busy people and they are following a marking scheme. Mostly they are looking to find out how well you've passed the Tutor Marked Assignment (TMA) or End of Module Assessment (EMA). So you need to make it as easy as possible for them to give you the best mark possible for the work you've done.

There are six easy to follow steps to this.

1. Read the question and answer it.
This one is obvious, but if you read feedback from tutors shows that it doesn't always get followed. Not doing this makes you fail.

The time to read the question is before you start working through the relevant course material. TMAs are usually structured to follow the course material, often they specifically reference a unit.

If you have the EMA question at the start of the course then read it then. Otherwise read it as soon as it becomes available and plan your revision on how you answer the EMA. TMAs & EMAs are open book, so you have time to read the correct bit of the course material to help you answer.

DO read the question, get clues from it, and then answer exactly what is asked.

DON'T write the answer you hoped for.

2. Use the Whole Word Count

TMAs and EMAs have a word count limit, this always comes with a 10% leeway. You must use the whole word count, and some of the leeway.

Bank on writing as much as you need to answer each part of the question, and then trim it down on an edit when you are finished. The more quality information you get into the given word count the higher your mark can be. The material needs to be in there for the marker to find.

DO pay attention to the mark allocation for each question, your word count and time should reflect the marks available for each part.

3. Have a clear open structure

- Use bullet points where appropriate
- wide margins (2.5 – 3cm) & white space (break up paragraphs)
- 12 point font, 1.5 line spacing (more than x1, not as much as x2)

4. Sign post your answers

Make it very easy to scan the TMA/EMA.

Use headings for each part of a question that you answer. Be careful of multiple part questions, split out your answers to each part to ensure that a marker can just tick them off on their first read through.

use diagrams carefully (e.g. table for SWOT)

- annotate diagrams
- explain what you think they show

5. Use course material

Another obvious one. The OU, like all universities, wants you to demonstrate that you have learnt from the course material. Having read the question (see step 1 above) you should look for answers in the course material, either in theory to apply, or in the case studies.

Often there will be a case study of a very similar approach to the questions that are asked in a TMA or EMA that you can use to help you know what to include in your answers. At the very least this will give you a clue on where to look in the course material for theory.

When applying theory to an answer:

1. state the context
2. introduce the theory
3. apply the theory to the context
4. criticise the theory in context

6. Reference

This shouldn't need to be said. Make sure you reference appropriately. It helps to show that you:

- have read and absorbed the course material;
- give credit for others ideas; and
- for a distinction level have read further than the course material

If you have the time it is always worth reading the original ideas as referenced in the course material (and you can copy references from the course material if you need help with formatting them).

Often this gives you a different take on it from the course authors and helps you to back up any arguments you need to make to justify conclusions or opinions.

On Reflective Commentaries
18 January 2014

In finishing off TMA2 for the creative writing course I had a lightbulb moment. This was in response to some discussion on a student forum about how the marking didn't necessarily follow the quality of the submitted piece of writing.

The other student attributed this to the subjectiveness of 'good' writing. Or rather, that it is hard to mark the qualitative aspects of stories, poetry etc on an absolute scale.

Accepting that, and taking it from the university perspective. You need tutors to be consistent, and that leads to robust marking guidelines that are completely objective.

This then avoids valid criticism and legal challenges that could be successful. Both of the last are a bad thing from an organisational perspective, especially a university.

So what do you base these robustly objective marking guidelines on?
Answer: The course materials.

As a student the key is to cynically work in everything you have learnt from the course materials into your work. You probably also want to read the sources cited in the course books and then cite them directly too.

Remember that academics are citation snobs, the more you can go back to the original sources the better (and I've always found reading original papers rather than executive summaries written by others far better for understanding the subject).

What the markers want to know is that you have demonstrably learnt from doing the course, and that what you have demonstrably learnt has been because of the course materials rather than in spite of it. This is where the commentary comes in.

With the exception of a Mathematics course I did (MST121) all the other Open University course I've done so far (M865, B301, B629, A215, B120 & B203) all featured a commentary as part of the assignments. Typically these want 3-500 words on how you did the assignment.

Things for a good commentary

1. Don't simply report how you did the assignment, show how useful the course materials have been

2. Mention how you used every one of the main ideas in the relevant parts of the course so far (NB not just the bits the assignment seems to be about, you are supposed to keep on using the learning from the previous sections)

3. Show how you have gone beyond the course material to find more material from the library/other sources (NB you can refer to a Bibliography here if there is a lot of it not otherwise referenced. Bibliographies are outside the word count allowances, as are references and titles).

4.	If there is anything in the course material you haven't used in the main part of the assignment then mention why not (don't just say lack of space, be creative and compare its usefulness to the bits you did include)

5.	Consider writing the commentary at the beginning of the assignment, and do a draft of it as part of your planning

6.	Keep notes all the way through the assignment (and reading of course materials) that could help you to write the commentary

7.	Find someone you trust to read the draft for typos, grammatical errors etc (but not another course student because you don't want any hint at plagiarism).

I'm not guaranteeing that this will work and get you top marks, it's just some things I've observed over a few courses and that I am now trying to consciously apply myself in the writing of commentaries. For all I know it is complete bunk, I've never actually seen any marking guidelines.

Part 6 - On Publishing

18 - Experiments with self-publishing

Why Does My Book Not Sell?
20 October 2014

My rating: 5 of 5 stars

Rayne Hall's *Why Does My Book Not Sell?* is full of useful tips, and more importantly a broad framework for approaching improving your work as what works is continually evolving.

Once enough people find a new technique for improving their book's visibility and sales it becomes less useful. However there are definitely a set of things that will always remain useful.

I'm not going to tell you the list, Rayne deserves to profit from her hard work and she's not charging the earth for the book. I got it on pre-order for £0.77, about 99 cents US. That could of course just have been a ploy on her part to catapult it up the sales rankings. However even if it costs you a little more it may still be worth it for the advice.

Each of the things in the list is backed up with some evidence of Rayne's own experience, and some of them from other people. The explanations given seem sound to me, and there are a number of very sensible caveats about the fact that the market for books is ever changing and as more and more people try things then they become less effective.

If I was to sum up the advice it would be

- keep trying new things to make your work stand out from the crowd.
- You can use the top few best sellers as a sort of example, although beware that others may do the same thing and it may not help you.
- Do what works for you for as long as it works,
- keep on innovating and move on when things become less effective.

Seems sound advice for life.

There is a load more in there, and just reading it may help you think of more. Don't forget to look at things from your reader's point of view. Who do you think your target market is and how do they find new books?

One caveat from me though. I've not yet had time to update any of my own work, so I cannot say whether or not any of the advice in Rayne's book actually works for me. However I still think it was valuable to me as a writer for the reflection time it gave me when I read it.

Reader Perspectives
22 October 2014

Following on from my review of Rayne Hall's book about ways to increase your book sales I thought I might spend a few minutes reflecting on how I, as a reader, find new books to read.

What do I read?
You can see the details over on my Goodreads shelf, my 2014 Challenge was to read 50 books this year (numerically slightly down on last year, but 12 parts of John Scalzi's Human Division counted as 12 on goodreads when it was really just a single serialised novel (and I really enjoyed it).

My reading is divided into three broad categories,

- I read easy fiction for escape and enjoyment,
- histories for a better understanding of why and how we got here, and
- course related material for the Open University degree that I am doing.

Typically the heavier the degree module I'm on the less history gets read and the more the lighter fiction creeps in.

Recent Reading
Over the last year I've read a number of series, these have included Ben Aaronovitch's Rivers of London series (I started it from a comment recommending it made by Charlie Stross on his blog).

The first one was put on my wishlist when I saw the comment, in the end I bought it second hand in paperback in the run up to Christmas. Because I really liked it the rest of the series were bought for the kindle and read standing on the train when I couldn't get a seat to write. I only did this because their kindle price was below my threshold. I have the newest volume on pre-order in hardback, its due out in November and I expect to read it within a couple of weeks.

I also read Elizabeth Moon's Vatta's War series. Again I saw a recommendation somewhere, I think it was a discussion of the Bechdel Test and someone listed some space opera with a female protagonist. Again no.1 went on the wishlist and was procured secondhand in paperback.

The kindle prices were more than the used paperbacks so the rest of the series went onto my wishlist and arrived for Christmas and birthdays. I finally read the last one of these in September (after a long break). I'd read more of this, but I haven't gone actively looking for similar stuff.

Some of the reviews I read were mixed, and suggested that there were strong similarities between series and characters across other books by the Elizabeth Moon. This hasn't put me off, I just haven't had time to go looking for more.

There are a few authors where I automatically buy their next book, although not many. Iain Banks was one, although alas no more. Terry Pratchett is another, as is

Neil Gaiman, Charles Stross and now Ben Aaronovitch. When these guys release a book I usually have it on pre-order and it gets read shortly after it arrives.

They get on the list by consistently producing books that I like. In the past David Eddings has been on it (I just don't recall seeing anything new from him for a long while) and so was George Macdonald Fraser. John Scalzi is getting there too, as is Cory Doctorow.

The reason this list is so short though is because most of my reading isn't fiction. It's history, and I read this by period, and often following a specific thread. For example, I like to read first hand accounts of British service personnel.

More recently what I have been collecting works on is SOE operations in France in 1942-44. So I've found all the books I can, read the bibliographies and looked for those too. Nearly all of these go on wish lists for Christmas/Birthday presents, especially the expensive or rare ones.

Where do I find new titles?

In no particular order

- Recommendations from people I know/trust
- randomly browsing in charity shops
- Amazon's kindle daily deals
- requests to review books

A low price means that I will randomly pick things up and buy them if they look even vaguely interesting. I've discovered in almost two years of owning a kindle that there is a limit to the number of titles you can hold on it (200 titles, but it seems to be a database/display constraint rather than storage space).

If you read the blog you'll have noticed that I review most of the books that I read. I also post those reviews both on amazon.co.uk and Goodreads. I currently have an Amazon reviewer rank of 3,880. This means that sometimes I get emails from people asking if I'll review something in return for a free review copy.

Mostly I say no, because generally they've offered me something I don't want, but sometimes I get offered an interesting book. In those cases I always say yes.

Buying ebooks
I don't like paying more than about £3 for a kindle edition. I appreciate the work still goes into it, but my value psychology (which is similar to most people in operation if not in numerical value) is that I cannot spend money on intangibles.

How about you? How do you find new books to read, and what prompts you to buy/not buy a given title?

A/B Testing Amazon book sales
26 January 2015

A/B Testing is when you try two almost identical approaches out with real people to see which option gets the best response. The only difference between A & B is the thing that you are trying to test.

In my trial I had the same science fiction novella available through two Amazon ASIN. Both were enrolled in KDP (there's nothing forbidding this but I'm sure Amazon don't encourage that behaviour).

- Crisis Point (UK – 2 (5☆) reviews)
- Crisis Point (UK – 0 reviews)

What was different between these two was that one of the versions has two reviews, both five stars. There are also changes to the wording in the blurb.

The test
So this wasn't quite true A/B Testing as I didn't perform the free days simultaneously, one was over the Christmas period and the other was last weekend. However both versions got the same twitter announcements from me.

I scheduled a number of tweets giving a mixture of links to the UK, US, Canadian and Australian amazon links. The key difference on these was that for the reviewed version I mentioned it as having five stars.

One thing that the reviewed version hasn't had, but the unreviewed version does, is some paid twitter advertising. This gets it five tweets a day from different accounts with a seven day cycle of tweet content. So it has had more advertising for a period of a month before I started the free days for the version with reviews.

Results

Despite lots of pushing the unreviewed version only got 18 downloads when it was free. Given that this was 24-29 Dec when I figured lots of people would be looking for stuff to put on their new kindle it seems pretty poor.

The version with two five star reviews and slightly less publicity beat the other one for free downloads within six hours. There was also a paid download in the period between the first tweet and it becoming free.

Conclusions

- Reviews are needed to sell books, even when you are giving them away!
- Don't pay for advertising until you've got some good reviews behind your book.

Thoughts on Commercial Success
13 May 2015

Not a how to but just some reflections based on the things that I have read recently that seem to be successful. I doubt this will help anyone sell more books.

'In' groups
A number of the apparently successful stories have groups of characters that follow a defining characteristic. For example Harry Potter has the four houses, Divergent has factions, Game of Thrones has noble houses, Hunger Games has it too in the way the districts have their specialist industries.

Readers can see themself in one or more of these in groups and can feel that they could live in the fictional world. This helps to get emotional attachment and makes it more likely that they will get shared socially.

Part of this is in the characters too, all of those books have a range of characters that people can relate to. That's not all people to all characters, but that most people will be able to relate to at least one of the primary characters in the story. That's a great hook.

Young Adult target
Almost everything I've mentioned above is targeted at young people, some more explicitly than others. The Twilight series is another example of this.

Young people (i.e. those under 25) are more likely to be working out what they like to read, they're also more likely to share what they find. It's a generational thing about how they do this, but not that they do. Social life where you get to discuss stuff and share in person tends to drop off when kids come along.

The Power of Free
21 July 2013

So having spent some time thinking on it I have decided two things.

1. That *Exodus: Perfects* is the best start to the series (it starts the main arc of the story).
2. That obscurity is the biggest threat to being an author.

So given both 1 & 2 above the solution is a more or less permanently free ebook of *Exodus: Perfects*. Now that the exclusivity of *Exodus: Perfects* to Amazon has expired I can make it available through other sources. (NB this is the novella that eventually became the novel *Perfects*).

Free Ebook on Amazon Kindle
When you sign up for Kindle Direct Publishing (KDP) it offers you a 90 day tie in to their KDP Select programme, which allows you to give your title away for free 5 days out of 90. At first sight it seems to be the only way to make your book free for any period of time, other than just dropping it on a website.

That last option would work, but will shift significantly fewer copies and is still prone to obscurity. Also, when you use a large distributor you get data on the number of people that have downloaded your book.

Ebook publishing on Smashwords

However what I subsequently discovered is that Amazon will price match. Also, other places can sell your ebook for you, or rather give people a free ebook.

This means that Amazon will also (hopefully) give people a free ebook. So I went for smashwords. There's a reason why I chose them though, partly they came with good recommendations, and partly they're one of the few distributors that covers everything Amazon doesn't.

Smashwords will distribute your ebook to Apple, Google, Barnes & Noble and a host of others (although you do need an ISBN for the full range).

Why a free ebook?

There's a major difference in the rate at which people will download a free ebook against a very cheap (minimum price $0.99 US or £0.77).

A handful of people will pay you for a novella from an unknown author (some people bought mine), but hundreds will download a free ebook. OK, the people who pay are very likely to actually read it, much more so than the hundreds that download it for free. However, if someone has your book on their e-reader then there is a chance, albeit small, that they'll read it, enjoy it, and leave a review somewhere.

Anyway, it's a theory that's worth a spin. I don't write with the intent of making money from it. I write because I enjoy writing, and what makes it enjoyable, is the idea that other people might like my stories.

19 - Editing

Editing Perfects

27 July 2015

Over the last few weeks I've been editing Perfects for a second draft. I finished it over two years ago and it has sat in the metaphorical drawer waiting until I had time between uni courses to focus on it and apply what I learned from A215 to it.

As a re-cap, Perfects is an evolution of Exodus, which was my multi-threaded NaNoWriMo 2012 story of a mid twenty first century exodus of people from Earth into space as space travel became an order of magnitude cheaper. I decided when I re-looked at it that there was an interesting world there, but that the strands needed loads of work to knit together.

One of the strands became the novella Crisis Point, which I released in 2013. Perfects followed a group of genetically engineered teenagers and twenty-somethings living mainly in Cambridge.

Their world is one where their creation was unlawful and their existence is stigmatised. I worked it up into a much longer story in 2013 and then parked it when I signed up for the Open University undergrad creative writing course.

With a couple of years worth of hindsight applied I can see from my editing process that it is very much a rough diamond. It's a good story but there's quite a bit of polishing to be done before I give it to anyone else to read, let alone pay for a professional editor.

I've knocked over twenty thousand words off the original first draft and put all the remaining scenes in a sensible order. I've also made some notes on a paper version about things I want to amend for narrative consistency. Lastly I've identified the need for a couple more scenes to ensure there is a coherence to the plot.

On top of all, that I will also be going back through each scene to ensure that it comes from the most appropriate point of view, the perspective is right, there is a good balance of show vs. tell and that it either drives the plot along or adds to the story. I've marked a couple of the ranty internal monologues either to convert to conversations or simply remove them to my personal character background notes.

My original intention had been to serialise the novel, and I released a couple of parts as novellas not long after I'd written them. This version is longer and complete, it also has an earlier start point that explains the situation better. The first scene also starts with a bang (actually it ends with the bang, but it starts with the highjacking of an orbital science facility).

Green Ink for happier editing?
26 August 2015

For almost two decades I have used green ink when commenting on documents and for editing. I've come to believe that green ink is the best colour for editing for a variety of reasons. Here they are.

Green is psychologically positive
Traditionally red ink has been used for correcting proofs. Red has a negative connotation, we use it for stop signs and prohibitions. Psychologically red can symbolise the blood from our work, and if there is a lot of red on the page then we get disillusioned and dispirited. So much so that UK civil service core competency framework has "wields the red pen" as an unacceptable trait for senior civil servants.

Green Ink carries the opposite connotations to red ink. We use green for go, and for affirming things. So green ink on the page doesn't carry the same emotional baggage that red ink does.

Green Ink is distinctive
Mostly when you buy pens in a non specialist shop you get a choice of black, blue or red. Lots of people stick to these colours. So they're normal. Green Ink isn't normal. Green ink stands out. Very well.

This makes it easier to read both the additions and the excisions. Most text is printed black on white. Green Ink is often lighter than the red equivalent and so you can read the original text even when you strike through it.

When there are multiple editors it can be easier to spot yours if you've used a different colour ink from the others.

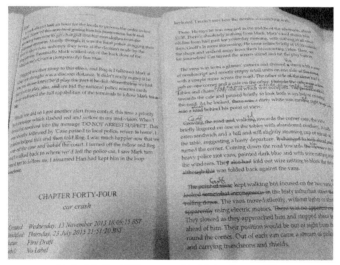

An example of Green vs Red ink when editing

How I found Green Ink

My own journey with green ink was serendipitous. I was part of an internal consultancy and we were separated from the rest of the directorate by an office move. We had no stationery cupboard and in urgent need of fresh pens I found a forgotten box of green Bic biros.

We used these for a bit, and in editing and proofreading the unit's reports we realised that the green ink was friendlier. Since then I've stuck to it as much as possible.

Other Users of Green Ink

In HM Treasury accounting guidance there used to be an index entry in the paper version about green ink. On following the reference there was a prohibition on green ink by finance teams as it was reserved for auditors.

In the armed forces only officers of General rank are permitted to use green ink. This is largely to ensure that their comments can be clearly identified. I'm uncertain whether this rule also applies within the MOD to its civil servants.

20 – Conclusions

A215 Creative Writing is done
18 July 2014

Last week I got the results for A215 Creative Writing. I got a Grade 2 pass, which I'm pleased with. So far I'm halfway through the degree and the level 2/3 courses that count towards Honours classification.

A215 has been the most interesting OU course that I have done so far. Part of me wishes that I could change from a business degree to English. However that's not going to happen, much as I might enjoy it.

Instead I will add A363 (Advanced Creative Writing) to my wishlist for when I've finished the BA in Business Studies. One day, closer to my retirement, I might do a proper BA in Humanities. I like to think I can do science and art!

A215 – Creative Writing
So here's my round-up of the Open University's Creative Writing course.

- it covers life writing, short fiction and poetry as forms, harnessing creativity, and editing & presenting your work
- there is an emphasis on giving and receiving feedback and writing to deadlines, also on lots

of drafts to continually improve on your work before submission

- it helps immensely if you keep a notebook to jot ideas down
- just write every day, even fantastic stuff starts as a rubbish first draft
- there are five Tutor Marked Assessments & an End of Module Assessment (i.e. not an exam)

Assessments

TMA1 is a free choice, very short and you can pretty much write what you like. The focus on this part of the module is getting your creativity flowing, and exercises to prompt you to write. The questions gives some prompts, which vary from year to year, but you can choose your own subject and form.

The assignment booklet is full of useful advice and suggestions for how to complete the assignment. The marking criteria for this assignment, representing 10% of the overall weight, seems laxer than later TMAs. You should use this TMA to get used to sharing your drafts with others.

TMA2 is short fiction, this is the one that you get the longest time to complete, later TMAs seem to get closer together, with four weeks between TMAs 3, 4, & 5. You need to have listened to the feedback on TMA1 here, practiced on student fora and made sure you get lots of feedback before you submit it.

If fiction is your thing you could try writing more than one so that you have the kernel of story ideas for both TMA5 and the EMA. I enjoy writing fiction the most, but I struggled with this because the word count was so tight, my stories tend to come out 2-3 times longer than this. This TMA is also worth 30% of the total score (all the others being 20% each).

TMA3 is poetry, you need to write 40 lines. Again there are some suggestions and prompts but you have a free choice. The course book was a bit rubbish on poetry, unless you'd done an English Lit module on poetry you'd be completely lost. Fortunately Stephen Fry's book *The Ode Less Travelled* is very good and easy to come by.

I also had a poet as my tutor and her day school on poetry was very valuable. I learnt the most in this section of the course. It was a big surprise to me that I could write poetry (and there are plenty of blog posts about this).

TMA4 is life writing, which is what I did for TMA1 as well. This is about understanding the blurring of boundaries between biography and fiction and how you can use a lot of techniques to explore human emotions and tell engaging stories. Life writing doesn't have to stick to the facts, nor should it be boring.

TMA5 is a free choice on form. The focus is doing research on getting your work published and producing something that edited and polished to a professional standard. Unlike the earlier TMAs there is a component in the commentary where you need to discuss the research you did and how you tailored your work to the publication that you chose.

My advice on this one is try to start it as early as possible, don't wait until you've finished TMA4.

The End of Module Assessment (EMA) comes round a month after TMA5. You really need to start on it about Easter if you want to do it justice. A longer piece than any of the TMAs it allows you to show off what you have learnt, and that is the emphasis on many OU courses, reflecting and showing that you have met the course objectives.

Unlike the TMAs it is marked twice and your score is the average of the two tutors marks. You also don't get the direct feedback with the results like you do for the TMAs. Your overall score is determined by both the EMA and the weighted TMAs.

Could You Write Five Million Words?
27 February 2015

Five million words.

That's about a hundred NaNoWriMo winners worth of words. More than most authors will publish in a lifetime. Yet it's not far off what you need to write to become a good writer.

Ten Thousand Hours
There's a theory, most famously expounded by Malcolm Gladwell in *Outliers*, that you need to spend about ten thousand hours practicing a skill before you get to the world class level. He cites The Beatles and Bill Gates amongst others as examples of this. There's more to success than just putting in the hours, but it certainly counts for a big chunk of it.

So what counts as practice as a writer?
You'd think this was obvious, writing stuff, and maybe a bit of reading. However I'd disagree with that, or rather modify it a bit. What I think makes you increase in skill as a writer is literacy, and time to reflect on what you read and write. But you need to reflect and think critically about it.

There's a big difference between doing the same hour ten thousand times and doing ten thousand hours of something. That said, there's no harm in repetition, after all that's the core of editing. But each iteration should try to be incrementally better.

When it comes to writing most of us have already had quite a lot of hours of relevant practice. About a fifth of primary school is spent on directly relevant literacy lessons. That's about 1,300 of the hours you need to start you off. There's about the same again in high school, assuming you attended and paid attention.

So most young adults have over a quarter of their ten thousand hours as a writer already in the bag. That's way more than even a keen wannabe pop star will have managed on finishing high school.

Five Million Words

Five Million Words isn't a random number. That's what ten thousand hours of me writing would produce, based on my current rate of output rather than an average over my life so far.

When I first did NaNoWriMo in November 2012 I kept a record of how long I spent writing each day as well as the total word count. There was a range of writing rates, but 90% of them were in the 30-40 words per minute range.

Taking the mid-point of 35 words per minute, it's within a single standard deviation of the median, mode and mean for the times I recorded. Also I've got faster since then, some of that is down to having completed an undergraduate creative writing course with the Open University.

You might have done some mental arithmetic there and gone, hang on, 35 words per minute over ten thousand hours is way more than five million words. You'd be right, it's about four times that.

But 35 words per minute is a typing speed, not a writing speed. It also doesn't account for time spent editing and re-writing. I've done a fair amount of that in the last two and a half years. I've also reflected on how I go about writing and understood how the creative process works for me.

I probably spend as much time thinking about a story and re-telling it to myself in my head before I put finger to keyboard. After I've left the keyboard and it has time to settle there is about the same time again on a couple of successive drafts to polish it and improve it. Often this loses words, so far I end up about 10-20% shorter (but some stories have halved).

So that's how I get from ten thousand hours to five million words.

How far have I got?
I'm not far off. My education probably accounts for about 3,000 hours. I did pay attention and I managed to get reasonable scores in my exams for English. I also went to university and wrote the odd essay or two (even though I mostly studied science).

I've also spent 22 years working as a civil servant, almost half of that has been spent in policy or strategy roles that have had very heavy writing components.

I've always considered that my early years in the civil service were where I learnt to write well. I had a three year period in an internal consultancy unit where I was coached by two separate managers with Firsts from Oxbridge colleges in English. I also edited and proofed about forty publications by the unit in that time (including writing about ten of those as the primary author and contributing to another twenty).

A number of other roles included writing for publication, including draft answers to Parliamentary Questions (a good PQ answer should be honest, accurate and demonstrably answer the question without being overly helpful) and media enquiries.

I'd score myself at least another 6,000 hours from this work, putting me at about 9,000 hours in total. From there I'm going to switch to word count for the rest. If 10k hours is 5 million words, then a thousand hours is half a million words. That's still a lot of words.

So far I've written 100k words for NaNoWriMo entries. I've also written another 50k in unpublished drafts of short stories, most of which have been edited to the point where they could be published.

There's also almost 200k words on this blog. So that's about 350k words. There's also some poetry, about three hundred lines of it, but I'm not sure how that equates in hours or words (poetry is much more time consuming, or at least I find it so). I also have a folder of hard copy first drafts from my teens and twenties that one day will get edited and digitised. As well as that there's material on my other websites and my contributions to usenet in the late 1990s, but I'm not going to go count those, nor my Open University assignments.

I'll probably produce about 150,000 more words to hit the ten thousand hours of creative writing time. I'm writing 2-3 blog posts a week, so I ought to get there sometime early in 2016.

The Secret of Success or Snake Oil?
23 September 2015

The Secret of Success is offered on many pages across the Internet. They're almost all snake oil salesmen trying to part you from your money with the temptation of an easy win. The real secret of success is there is no such thing as an easy win.

Secret of Success
I think that there are four elements to being successful. Here is the secret of success as I see it.

- work hard
- learn from failures
- perseverance
- get lucky

Why should you believe me? You've never heard of me as a big shot. Well that would be fair. In my chosen career, as a public servant, I'm moderately successful. I'm in the top 2% of UK civil servants. Not big enough for you have heard of, but successful enough to have worked out how the system works. I've also been studying leadership as part of a business studies degree. So I've spent some time looking at successful and unsuccessful people and companies.

What counts as success?
Frankly what you count as a success is up to you. Personally I count success as having a happy and fulfilled life. Money and the trappings of wealth or fame don't come into it. If you read about the people the

paparazzi follow you'll find many of them are unhappy in some way.

So think what your goals are and then work to get them. Another secret of success is that it is what you make it yourself.

Seven Habits
You might be aware of the seven habits of highly successful people. These pretty much work as another form of the secret to success.

The Secret of Success explained
You can only succeed by doing things. Opportunity knocks all the time, just very faintly. You need to work hard to make your own opportunities and then play them for all you can.

When they don't work out, don't be disheartened. Reflect on what you can learn from the experience. Apply that insight to the next opportunity you've made. That is the secret of success. Hard work and perseverance, along with the humility to learn from your mistakes.

References

These are some of the references I used for the various assignments during my Open University course. I have removed the references to postings in OU areas because these aren't things you will be able to access.

Anderson, L. (2006) *Creative Writing: A Workbook With Readings*, Milton Keynes, Open University NB - this is the Big Red Book

Browne, R. & King, D. (2004) *Self-Editing for Fiction Writers: How to edit yourself into print*, 2nd Edition, New York, Harper Collins

Fry, S. (2005), *The Ode Less Travelled*, London, Hutchinson

Granta (2014), 'Submissions' Granta Magazine, undated [online] Available at http://www.granta.com/submissions (accessed 30th April 2014)

Great Britain, (2013), *Immigration Rules - Part 1*, Home Office, November 2013, [online] available from: https://www.gov.uk/government/uploads/system/uploads/attachment_data/file/286238/Immigration_Rules_-_Part_1.pdf (accessed 3rd April 2014)

Kemp, J.M. (2012), Unpublished journal of an Immigration Officer at Gatwick South Note: I spent the summer of 2012 working as a contingency border officer during the Olympic period.

Rialto (2014), 'Poetry Submissions' The Rialto – the poetry magazine to read, undated [online] Available at http://www.therialto.co.uk/pages/about/the-magazine/submissions/ (accessed 30th April 2014)

Bibliography

Anderson, L. (2006) *Creative Writing: A Workbook With Readings*, Milton Keynes, Open University

Braddon, R. (1989) Woman in Arms, Glasgow, Armada

Helm, S. (2006) A Life in Secrets: The Story of Vera Atkins and the Lost Agents of SOE, London, Abacus

Kramer, R. (2011) Flames in the Field: the story of four SOE agents in occupied France, kindle edition, Penguin

National Archives. (2004) SOE Syllabus: Lessons in ungentlemanly warfare, World War II, Bury St Edmunds, St Edmundsbury Press

Ruby, M. (1990) F Section SOE, Glasgow, Grafton

Granta 82, *Life's Like That*

Granta 118, *Exit Strategies*

Granta 125, *After the War*

Kreibich, C., 'Spamalytics, An empirical analysis of spam marketing conversion' 10 June 2013, http://www.icir.org/christian/spamalytics/ (accessed 27 April 2014).

Fry, S. (2005), *The Ode Less Travelled*, London, Hutchinson

About the Author

James Kemp has been writing stories for over 30 years, sometimes he has even written (non-fiction) for a living.

For more of his writing you could have a look at his blog at or his facebook page. You can also sign up to receive very occasional news on new releases and special offers at http://www.themself.org/books

If you liked the story, please leave a review, or at least rate it, on Amazon, Goodreads or wherever you bought it from. If you thought there was room for improvement, then he'd love to hear from you.

Blog: http://www.themself.org/
Twitter: @greencoatboy
Facebook: http://www.facebook.com/jamesmkempauthor

That's all. Thanks for reading.

Printed in Great Britain
by Amazon

56833247R00139